Evelyn Hooker

and the

Fairy Project

Magination Press

Books for Kids From the
American Psychological Association

Magination Press is a registered trademark of the American Psychological
Association. Order books at maginationpress.org, or call 1-800-374-2721.

Book design by Rachel Ross
Cover printed by Phoenix Color, Hagerstown, MD
Interior printed by Sheridan Books, Inc., Chelsea, MI

Library of Congress Cataloging-in-Publication Data
Names: Pitman, Gayle E., author. | Green, Sarah, illustrator.
Title: Evelyn Hooker and the fairy project / by Gayle E. Pitman;
[illustrated by Sarah Green].
Description: Washington, DC: Magination Press, [2021] | Summary:
"This biography tells the story of Evelyn Hooker, the woman behind
the research, advocacy, and allyship that led to the removal of the
"homosexuality" diagnosis from the Diagnostic and Statistical Manual of
Mental Disorders"—Provided by publisher.
Identifiers: LCCN 2020057230 (print) | LCCN 2020057231 (ebook) | ISBN
9781433830471 (hardcover) | ISBN 9781433836961 (ebook)
Subjects: LCSH: Hooker, Evelyn Caldwell—Juvenile literature. |
Psychologists—Biography—Juvenile literature. | Homosexuality—
Juvenile literature. | Mental illness—Classification—Juvenile literature.
Classification: LCC BF109.H66 P58 2021 (print) | LCC BF109.H66 (ebook) |
DDC 150.92 [B]—dc23
LC record available at https://lccn.loc.gov/2020057230
LC ebook record available at https://lccn.loc.gov/2020057231

Manufactured in the United States of America
10 9 8 7 6 5 4 3 2 1

Evelyn Hooker
— and the —
Fairy Project

by Gayle E. Pitman, PhD
illustrated by Sarah Green

Magination Press • Washington, DC
American Psychological Association

Note to Reader

Language is fluid, and the terminology used to describe sexual orientation has evolved over time to be more specific and respectful. It will likely continue to evolve after the publication of this book.

During Evelyn's time, gay men were called "homosexual(s)" and sexual behavior between people of the same sex was called "homosexuality." These broad terms reduce people's identities to their sexual behavior and are associated with negative stereotypes and discriminatory attitudes. Today we would say "gay men" when describing the gay men Evelyn worked with and lesbian, gay, straight, asexual, bisexual, queer, polysexual, or pansexual, for example, to describe a person's sexual orientation. People with these diverse identities have always existed, but the reporting, discourse, and studies in Evelyn's time were focused nearly exclusively on the concept of "homosexuality," and usually centered on gay men. Therefore this book does necessarily use labels like "homosexual" and "homosexuality" in a historical context, and refers mostly to "gay people" or "gay men," rather than the diverse array of identities we appreciate today.

However you may identify, once you leave this book, we encourage you to use respectful terms for accurate identities and orientations. It's the first step in being an ally or activist and recognizes your commitment to a fair and just world. As long as your heart and mind is open and you continue to do your research, learn, support, and advocate, it's OK if you make mistakes; we all do from time to time.

Your friends at Magination Press

TABLE OF CONTENTS

Chapter 1

Nebraska to California

Our story begins in North Platte, Nebraska, where Evelyn Hooker was born and spent part of her childhood. Hundreds of years before she was born, Native Americans inhabited a wide swath of the American prairie, including what is now North Dakota, South Dakota, Wyoming, Montana, Iowa, Oklahoma, Kansas, and Nebraska. Some were nomadic hunters, following the buffalo herds along the rich grasslands on horseback. Others were farmers, living in earth structures along the Platte River. The Lakota, one of three Sioux nations, lived in the area near North Platte.

1

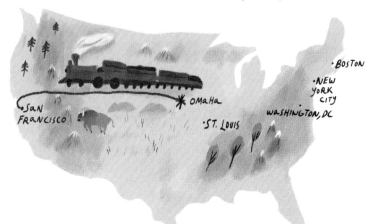

In the 1860s, everything changed. The building of the Transcontinental Railroad was underway. Railroad workers traveled from Omaha, Nebraska, to Promontory Summit, Utah, building temporary pop-up towns along the way. The men in these towns spent their days building the railroad, and entertained themselves at night by gambling, getting drunk in the makeshift saloons, and generally being rowdy and disorderly. When the work was finished, the men would pack up, roll their "Hell on Wheels" out of town, and move on to the next location. North Platte, Nebraska, was one of these "Hell on Wheels" towns.

The Native American nations that lived in the path of the railroad were not happy about this. Their land was being intruded upon without their permission, and there were many conflicts and clashes between the native people and the European railroad workers. As European travelers moved westward, thousands of native people were displaced, died of diseases like tuberculosis, cholera, and smallpox, or were killed. Eventually, these Native American homelands were lost altogether, and the people were forced onto reservations.

Two famous residents of North Platte highlight this history. Red Cloud, a member of the Lakota Sioux nation, was born along the forks of the Platte River. He was opposed to westward expansion and the appropriation of Native American lands by the Europeans. Over his lifetime, he and other Native American leaders tried to defend the land. In 1866–1868 they lead a successful campaign in Wyoming and Montana known as Red Cloud's War. But Red Cloud's long-term efforts were not so successful. Eventually, Red Cloud was stripped of his title as chief, and his people were forced to relocate to the Pine Ridge Reservation in South Dakota.

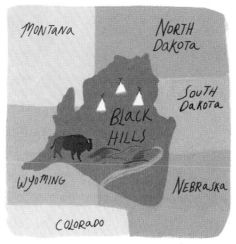

William Frederick Cody, more famously known as "Buffalo Bill," was another famous resident of North Platte. Born in Iowa Territory in 1846, he rode for the Pony Express as a kid, and he later fought for the Union Army in the Civil War. Later, he hunted buffalo for the Kansas Pacific Railroad workers, earning the nickname "Buffalo Bill." In 1883, after the completion of the Transcontinental Railroad and the relocation of Native Americans onto reservations, he formed "Buffalo Bill's Wild West," a traveling Western show headquartered on his ranch near North Platte. These shows romanticized the American frontier, featuring bucking broncos, shoot-'em-up displays, and celebrity performances by people like Annie Oakley, Lillian Smith, and Calamity Jane. The show typically ended with a performance of a Native American attack on a settler's cabin, and Buffalo Bill and his cowboys would ride in and protect them.

Evelyn Hooker was born in her grandmother's tiny house in North Platte on September 2, 1907, two years before Red Cloud's death. Buffalo Bill died 10 years later, in 1917.

This Is the Land

This is the land
where the river ambled through the verdant hills
where bison thundered across the golden plains
and Great Spirit watched over the people.
This is the land.

This is the land
where a herd of prairie schooners thundered
where men pitched their tent saloons and gambling houses
and, free from the watchful eyes of women, went feral.
This is the land.

This is the land
where Buffalo Bill launched his tawdry Western circus
where Calamity Jane dressed as a man
and Lillian Smith dressed as a princess.
This is the land.

This is the land
where one-room shacks littered the countryside
where tenant farmers struggled to eke out a living
and babies were born, one of whom would change the world.
This is the land.

Evelyn grew up in a small shack with her eight sisters and brothers. Her parents were tenant farmers, meaning that they paid rent to live on and farm the land. Many poor people living in rural areas in the early 1900s were either tenant farmers or sharecroppers (people who didn't pay rent, but who farmed the land in exchange for a portion of the crops they harvested). It was common for tenant farmer families to have lots of children, because even though there were more mouths to feed and bodies to clothe, the children could work on the farm and help the family earn a better living. For the first 12 years of her life, Evelyn's family moved from farm to farm, trying to make ends meet.

Because Evelyn's family moved frequently, she attended a succession of one-room schoolhouses. These schoolhouses were the only places where Evelyn could find books to read. There were no public libraries back then, and her family couldn't afford to purchase books. She savored every book she could get her hands on. Most children attending these rural schools learned little more than reading, writing, and basic arithmetic, and they typically left after the third or fourth grade in order to help their families earn money. Evelyn, however, was different.

Evelyn's mother, who had come to Nebraska as a child via covered wagon, didn't go to school past the third grade. Yet she valued education, and she saw the potential in Evelyn. Throughout Evelyn's childhood, her mother said, "Get an education and they can never take it away from you." These weren't empty words; when Evelyn was ready for high school, her mother moved the entire family to Sterling, Colorado, where there was a good-quality high school.

Evelyn was used to engaging in rote memorization, recitation, and repetition in school. In contrast, Sterling High School, a "Progressive School," emphasized problem-solving, critical thinking, and learning by doing. Evelyn thrived at Sterling, and in her senior year, her teachers talked her out of merely applying to a teacher's college and instead convinced her to apply to the University of Colorado. It was highly uncommon for women to attend college in the 1920s (let alone a large university), and those who did typically came from wealthy families. The idea of a young daughter of poor tenant farmers attending a large university was unheard of. But Evelyn earned a scholarship, and she enrolled in the university in the fall of 1924.

Evelyn knew from an early age what it felt like to be the target of prejudice. She undoubtedly felt stigmatized because of her family's poverty. She may have felt like an outsider because of her intellect, her interest in reading, and her success in school. She was also very self-conscious about her height; by age 13, she was nearly six feet tall, towering over her classmates. Many years later, Evelyn shared in an interview that one of the things that fueled her interest in studying gay men was her childhood experience of feeling different.

࿋

SUFFRAGE IS PROCLAIMED! U.S. WOMEN GET VOTE

The 19th Amendment, which was ratified in 1920, was a game-changer for women. The right to vote opened the door to a new range of opportunities. It also gave a massive boost to the concept of the "New Woman," a woman who exercised her agency and independence rather than conforming to strict gender expectations. Magazines and silent films were flooded with images of the "flapper," considered at the time to be the physical embodiment of female liberation. The short bobbed haircuts, dramatic makeup, and cocktail-length sheath dresses were a direct challenge to the constrictions of Victorian-era corsets and high-buttoned blouses. And behind the style was plenty of substance—women could pursue an education, get a job, and earn their own money.

Morning

Light filtered through the flimsy curtains.
The cries of young children pierced the air.
She couldn't suppress her sigh,
heavy with defeat.

She splashed grayish basin water on her face
and as she pulled her faded dress over her head
she noticed yet another tear to be mended
just like the one she'd fixed yesterday.

She bundled her hair like sheaves of wheat,
picked up her basket,
and headed to town,
gripping her young with her gnarled hands.

Miles they walked down a long, dusty path,
the sound of coins jangling in her pouch.
She prayed her children wouldn't ask for a peppermint stick.
Her answer was always the same.

She heard the voices
and felt the energy
in the distance
long before they arrived.

"Have you heard the news?" someone cried,
waving a newspaper
that cost more
than she could afford.

When she came home
she saw her mirror image working in the field
and thought about how things could be different
for her.

Later,
she sat down next to her and said
she would give her
something they could never take away from her.

*The poem "Morning" is inspired by Jessie Berthel,
whose freedom and independence were limited, like
many other women's, by poverty, limited opportunities
for women, and a lack of education.*

Women also had pioneering role models available to them. Amelia Earhart was the first woman to fly across the Atlantic. Margaret Sanger started what we now know as Planned Parenthood clinics, giving women the freedom to make decisions about family planning. Writers like Charlotte Perkins Gilman, Gertrude Stein, Dorothy Parker, and Edna St. Vincent Millay incorporated feminist themes into their novels, short stories, and poetry.

Changes were happening for other groups of people too. Many African Americans in the 1920s left rural areas and flocked to cities like New York and Chicago, giving rise to the Harlem Renaissance and the Jazz Age. These cities became cultural centers for African Americans, attracting writers, poets, dancers, musicians, artists, singers, and actors. Women like Zora Neale Hurston, Josephine Baker, Billie Holiday, and Bessie Smith were central figures

New Woman

What could a "new woman" of the 1920s do?
She could vote.
She could earn a high school diploma.
She could go to college.
She could have short hair.
She could wear a short skirt.
She could write books.
She could play music.
She could dance.
She could sing.

She could stay single.
She could get married.
She could get divorced.
She could wait to have children.
She could work outside the home.
She could be a doctor.
She could be a lawyer.
She could be a politician.
She could be a scientist.
She could ride a bicycle.
She could drive a car.
She could fly an airplane.
She could do anything.
Almost.

in the Harlem Renaissance. All of this was part of the "Great Migration," spanning from about 1920 until the Great Depression.

Not every woman had these opportunities, though. Many women didn't have the money to attend college or move to urban areas. Women of color were far more likely to work because they needed the money, not because they were exercising any freedoms. And the work they did—like domestic work, farm work, or factory work—was back-breaking. Middle-class married women were expected to stay home and care for children and their household. For them, going to school and getting a paid job outside the home wasn't an option.

Evelyn was of college age at a critical time in American history. Had she been born a generation earlier, she probably would not have finished high school or attended college. Evelyn's intelligence, coupled with a supportive mother and encouraging teachers, gave her an extra boost, earning her a scholarship to the University of Colorado. However, she still didn't have it easy, and she still experienced sexism. Because her scholarship didn't cover all of her expenses, Evelyn worked as a nanny for a wealthy family in Boulder, Colorado, while juggling her schoolwork. Even with these added responsibilities, Evelyn excelled in school, and after earning both her bachelor's and her master's degrees in psychology at the University of Colorado, she planned to apply to the PhD program in psychology at Yale University. However, the chair of the psychology department at the University of Colorado, who had attended Yale himself, refused to recommend Evelyn for admission. Why? Because she was a woman. She instead applied to the Johns Hopkins University in Baltimore, Maryland, where she became one of 11 women admitted to their PhD program.

Many years later, Evelyn retold the story of the psychology department chair's refusal to grant her a recommendation to Yale, saying, "This, from a man who studied why raccoons wash their food!" She was likely amused and irritated by this, wondering how on earth his research could have made any kind of positive impact in the world!

Research Career

The research question:
Why do raccoons wash their food?
This earned him tenure.

Sonnet

Oh, what a joy to breathe the summer air!

To luxuriate in the sanguine light

its amber tinted rays a morning prayer,

each beam a yearning for a future bright.

My eyes grow heavy into dreamlike bliss

I soon drift towards oblivious retreat.

The desert sun brands with its searing kiss

consuming me in its wildfire of heat.

But my sweetest delusion has gone pale

much like my pallid face, ashen and gray.

Once full of life, I'm now hauntingly frail.

This crass affliction hastens my decay.

Every time I gasp for a choking breath

I pray I'm not about to face my death.

TUBERCULOSIS, OR VICTORIAN CONSUMPTION

It was one of the hottest trends of the 1800s. All the A-list celebrities had it. It dictated the hottest style trends of the Victorian era—tiny waists, wide glistening eyes, snow-white skin, red lips, rosy cheeks. Back then, "tuberculosis chic" was all the rage.

It sounds completely bizarre, but it was true. Tuberculosis, also known as "consumption," "wasting disease," and "the White Plague," was a serious worldwide pandemic during the 1800s and early 1900s. During the Victorian era, before doctors knew what caused it, people believed that tuberculosis was a disease of the rich, famous, and artistic, and that it amplified the artistic passions of its victims. Many artists, writers, poets, and musicians, including Frederic Chopin, Jane Austen, Henry David Thoreau, Elizabeth Barrett Browning, Paul Gauguin, and John Keats died of the disease, and many more suffered from it and recovered. Victorian art and poetry was filled with images of frail, ghostly-looking women lying on dainty bed linens in white dressing gowns. The reality of tuberculosis was far less romantic, though. By the 1900s, more than 100,000 people per year in the US died from the disease, often as a result of choking on one's own bloody coughs.

By the turn of the century, scientists had discovered that tuberculosis was in fact caused by a bacterium, and not by one's artistic passions. At that point, the disease stopped being fashionable. It was also discovered that some of the hallmarks of Victorian style may well have been contributing to the epidemic. Corsets made it hard to breathe, long sweeping skirts picked up dirt, and being significantly underweight made recovery much more difficult. Patients began retreating from society, partly because they were stigmatized, and partly because the disease was so contagious. People with money found refuge and privacy in fancy sanatoriums, many of which were sprouting up in desert areas like Colorado, New Mexico, Arizona, and California. The dry air and hot temperatures in these areas were considered to be essential healing elements. Patients spent their days in beds lined up on open-air verandas and porches, soaking up as much sun and fresh air as they could. Sanatoriums continued to provide respite to tuberculosis patients until the 1950s, after vaccines and antibiotics had been developed to prevent and treat the disease.

Evelyn was one of those afflicted with tuberculosis during the sanatorium era. After earning her PhD in experimental psychology in 1932, she got a teaching job at the Maryland College for Women, despite the fact that at the height of the Great Depression, there weren't very many jobs available. She wasn't there long, though; in 1934, Evelyn was stricken with tuberculosis, and with the support and financial help of friends, she went to a sanatorium in California. During her two years there, she spent her time reading, sitting out in the sun, and reflecting. She became keenly aware of her vulnerability, realizing that she wasn't invincible. But her recovery also helped her recognize how strong and resilient she was—qualities she would draw upon throughout her career.

After she recovered, Evelyn decided to stay in California, and she got a job at Whittier College in Southern California. She stayed there for a year, then had an opportunity that would change her life forever.

ﾒ

THE FÜHRER IS AT THE BAHNHOF!

Evelyn heard the chants in the streets, and knew it was her cue to go outside and watch. She went outside and met up with her friend Lucci. Both of them were in Berlin on a fellowship, studying clinical psychology at the Institute for Psychotherapy. Evelyn had taken a leave of absence from her teaching job at Whittier College to learn more about psychological disorders, diagnosis, and treatment—things that weren't part of her experimental psychology curriculum at Johns

Hopkins. It was March 1938, a few days after Germany took over Austria, and Adolf Hitler (the Führer, which means "leader") had just arrived at the train station (bahnhof). Everyone awaited Hitler's arrival at the Reich Chancellery, which was his official residence and headquarters. Evelyn was not a fan of Hitler or his totalitarian regime. She'd read in American newspapers about what the Nazis were doing—from burning books and spreading propaganda to driving Jewish people out of their jobs and beating them in the streets. But she also knew that any time Hitler's appearance was announced, you had to go outside and watch, or the Nazis would shoot you.

Evelyn and Lucci stood below the Reich Chancellery, which was decorated with flags bearing the swastika, the official Nazi symbol. The streets were filled with people eagerly anticipating Hitler's arrival. Hitler was popular in Germany, and the fact that Austria would now be a part of Germany made him even more popular. The crowd watched Hitler arrive at the Chancellery by motorcade. When Hitler appeared on the balcony, the crowd roared, and Evelyn watched in horror as everyone's hand shot up in the air—including Lucci's! Evelyn smacked her arm down and hissed, "Lucci! What do you think you're doing?" The Nazi salute was a sign of obedience and loyalty to Hitler and the Nazi party,

Why Did You Raise Your Arm?

(March 1938)

Because they told me to.
Because everyone else was doing it.
Because I didn't want people to judge me.
Because I got caught up in the energy of the moment.
Because I wasn't thinking straight.
Because I forgot where I was for a minute.
Because my brain was playing tricks on me.
Because I'm a terrible person.
Because they would shoot me if I didn't.

and Evelyn couldn't believe that her friend—a Quaker who believed in peace and was against violence—had automatically raised her arm. Lucci's behavior showed how easy it is to mindlessly obey an authority figure, even if that means going against what you believe is right and just.

\/

CRASH!!! BANG!!! BOOM!!!

The sounds of breaking glass shattered the nighttime quiet. Smoke filled the air, and people were screaming in the streets. What was going on?

Evelyn stayed with a Jewish family during her time in Berlin. Under the Nazi regime, life had become increasingly difficult for Jewish people, and Evelyn saw how it was impacting her host family. But on November 9 and 10, she witnessed something she never could have imagined—a massive riot against the Jewish community. The night of November 9, Nazi paramilitary forces raided and vandalized Jewish homes, businesses, synagogues, and schools. They smashed windows of Jewish-owned businesses, set synagogues on fire, and raided the homes of Jewish families. Thirty thousand Jewish men were rounded up, loaded up onto trucks, and sent to concentration camps. Hundreds of Jewish people were assaulted or killed, and the violence continued into the next day. This night of violence, which occurred throughout Germany, Austria, and Czechoslovakia, came to be known as "Kristallnacht," which means

Kristallnacht *(November 9, 1938)*

thousands of glittering shards raining down
sharp enough to pierce
the hearts
of our
people
leaving nothing but icy fragments
sprinkled with the blood
of a shattered community

"night of crystal," referencing the shards of broken glass that covered the streets.

What triggered this? Two days earlier, on November 7, a Polish Jewish man named Herschel Grynszpan shot a German diplomat in Paris named Ernst vom Rath. The news media in Germany, which was controlled by the Ministry of Public Enlightenment and Propaganda, blamed the Jewish people in general for vom Rath's murder. This was the Ministry's job: to glorify Adolf Hitler and his regime, to promote loyalty to the Nazi party, and to advance anti-Semitism. The Nazis saw the murder as a golden opportunity; they could now escalate their efforts against the Jewish people, and in their minds, they had the perfect justification for it. Nazi propaganda said "Jews are Communists. Jews are dangerous. Jews are murderers." These were the messages the Nazis were feeding people, and they were chillingly effective.

The night of Kristallnacht, Evelyn watched the parents of her host family try to console their young daughter. "I don't want to be Jewish anymore," the girl said. It was likely the night that her childhood was taken away from her, and it certainly signaled the final shattering of Jewish existence in Germany.

A few days after Kristallnacht, Jewish children were banned from schools, and by the end

Blacklisted

They put me on their blacklist
I've been summarily dismissed
because of what I've witnessed.
The death of free expression
the violent aggression
political suppression
all in the name of purity.
They promised their security
by fading a community
into complete obscurity.
They classified them
nullified them
terrified them
crucified them
then justified their hate
as ways to liberate
their totalitarian state.
They mutilated
decimated
fumigated
obliterated.
And now the hate is perpetuated
by these institutions
worrying about Final Solutions.
But I'm under no delusion
It's time for revolution.
Because of what I've witnessed
I won't be summarily dismissed
or put on anyone's
blacklist.

of November, the Nazis began to impose curfews. Anyone who violated these curfews could be arrested and taken to a concentration camp. By December, Jewish people were banned from most public places in Germany. Over 100,000 Jewish people fled in a panic during this time, seeking refuge in the United States, France, Belgium, the Netherlands, the United Kingdom, and Palestine. Most of the Jewish people who stayed in Germany perished in the concentration camps. Years after she left Berlin, Evelyn learned that the entire family she lived with met this fate.

All of these events strengthened Evelyn's resolve: whatever she did in her career, she wanted to make a difference for people who were oppressed. Before completing her fellowship, Evelyn went on a tour with English and American friends to Russia just after 1938. The year she spent in these two totalitarian states awakened her to the realities of social injustice, and she wanted to do whatever she could to create change.

Chapter 2

Unexpected Twists

After Evelyn returned from her fellowship in Berlin, she expected that her job at Whittier College would be waiting for her. But the timing was unfortunate. It was 1938, and fears of Communism were intensifying in the United States. The U.S. House of Representatives had just created the House Un-American Activities Committee (HUAC), whose job was to investigate people suspected of having Communist ties. College professors were among those who were targeted by the committee. Because colleges and universities have historically been places where people could share various points of view, debate political perspectives, and exercise academic freedom, college professors were prime targets of the HUAC.

Officials at Whittier had become suspicious of Evelyn, worrying that she'd absorbed the Nazi propaganda she'd been exposed to during her time in Berlin. Although she insisted that she was in no way a Nazi sympathizer, and that she'd witnessed terrible things during her stay, the college fired her from her job. Other faculty at Whittier were also dismissed for the same reason.

Stunned by her unexpected unemployment, Evelyn turned to her mentor from Johns Hopkins, Knight Dunlap. He was now the chair of the psychology department at the University of California, Los Angeles (UCLA), about 30 miles away from Whittier College. Dunlap sympathized with Evelyn, and said he wished he could give her a job. The department already had three female faculty members, though, and according to Dunlap, they were "cordially disliked." She was, however, offered a position as a teacher and research associate at UCLA's extension school, which offered courses to people who wanted to learn but weren't interested in getting a college degree. It was a less prestigious position, but it was a job. And it would turn out to be an important one; at UCLA, Evelyn met both her first husband, Donn Caldwell, and a student who would change her life forever. Evelyn quickly became popular among the students, many of whom were nontraditional students. They tended to be older, have full-time jobs, and be less financially well-off than the degree-seeking students at UCLA. Had she gotten the position on the main campus of the university, Evelyn probably wouldn't have met the student who ultimately convinced her to do her groundbreaking research.

Gay-dar

The way he walks.
The way he talks.
The way he sits.
The way he stands.
The way he's dressed.
The way he smells.
The way he chews.
The way he swallows.
The way he does his hair.
The way he moves his hands.
The way he holds his fork.
The way he sips his tea.
The way he looks at you.
The way he looks at me.
The way he kisses.
The way he hugs.
The way he shakes my hand.
The way he blushes.
They way he practically flew out the window.
That's how I know
he's queer.

HE WAS THE BRIGHTEST PERSON IN THE CLASS

That was what Evelyn later said about one of her students, a quiet, unassuming man named Sam From. A wisp of a person, Sam was the type of student who could sit in a classroom and go completely unnoticed. But despite his tiny frame and shy personality, he was the brightest star of the class. Sam's intellect made him memorable, and Evelyn was impressed by him. Sam often lingered after class for the opportunity to have a one-on-one conversation with Evelyn. When he learned that Evelyn took the streetcar home because of the wartime gas rationing, Sam offered to drive her home. That was the beginning of their long friendship.

Evelyn had a strict policy of not socializing with students out of class, and although she accepted rides home from Sam, she otherwise maintained her professional boundaries and didn't befriend him. However, once the semester ended, Sam reached out to Evelyn, and she invited him to visit her at her home. Her husband, Donn, had heard Evelyn talk about Sam, but he hadn't been formally introduced to him. Sam accepted the invitation, and they enjoyed a pleasant visit. After Sam left, Donn said to Evelyn, "You told me everything else about him. Why didn't you tell me he was queer?"

Evelyn was speechless. Queer? She'd never really thought about it, and Sam had never said anything to her. "How could you possibly know that?" she asked.

"Well," Donn countered, "he did everything but fly out the window!" A Hollywood screenwriter, Donn worked with many gay men*, and he was familiar enough with them to have a "sixth sense" about Sam.[1]

Before this, Evelyn hadn't really known anything about gay people, other than what she'd read in psychology textbooks. These accounts of gay people were typically very negative, characterizing them as immature, arrested in their development, sick, and deviant. After learning about Sam's sexual orientation, she became dismayed by the fact that she'd blindly accepted what was written in the textbooks without giving it a second thought.[2] Her opinion about sexuality began to change as Evelyn spent more time with her new friend.

Even though Evelyn knew Sam was gay, it took him a while to tell her. When Sam introduced Evelyn and Donn to his partner, George, he initially referred to him as his "cousin."

Once Sam was comfortable with Evelyn knowing the truth, he was eager to introduce Evelyn to his

---

*At one time gay men were called "homosexual(s)" and sexual behavior between people of the same sex was called "homosexuality." These terms are not acceptable today and are associated with negative stereotypes and discriminatory attitudes. This book uses updated language. However, when "homosexual" and "homosexuality" appears in this book, used in historical context or retained when referring to Evelyn's research. For more information, please read the Note to Reader at the beginning of this book.

gay friends. "She's another Eleanor Roosevelt!" he said with excitement. Eleanor Roosevelt was a good comparison—she had several close friends who were lesbians, and she was known for being accepting of gay and lesbian people despite the cultural stigmas of the era. "You've got to meet her." Sam took her to a house in downtown Los Angeles, and she was introduced to a group of poets, philosophers, engineers, and other intellectuals known as the "Benton Way Group," named for the street the house was on. Many of the people in this group were gay, and they accepted Evelyn as part of their group. Evelyn enjoyed a rare opportunity—to befriend a group of gay men and get to know them well.

⁕

SHOWTIME

It was a few minutes before 9 p.m., and the club was filled to capacity. Waiters scurried around taking last-minute drink orders. Then the house lights dimmed.

"Showtime!" bellowed the Master of Ceremonies, modeling a towering hairdo, sparkly eyeshadow, a sequined dress, and six-inch stilettos. Evelyn, Donn, Sam, and George sat back and took in the show.

Sam had invited Evelyn and Donn to travel with them to San Francisco for the Thanksgiving holiday.

Welcome to the Show!

Welcome, baby queen!
Is this your first time?
You're in for a past-your-bedtime
once-in-a-lifetime
come-back-anytime
night.

Who am I?
I'm a lip syncing
hard drinking
eye winking
heel clinking
QUEEN.

I'm a swaying hips
bright red lips
always looking for big fat tips
QUEEN.

I'm a catty
        batty
    fatty
            chatty
    bratty
            who's-your-daddy
QUEEN.

Some say I'm a demon
a she-man
a screamin' schemin' heathen.
They can stare and glare all they want
but I'm a hold-my-head-high,
walk with glide in my stride
QUEEN.

I'm a
super tramp
glitter vamp
sequined scamp
kicked out of band camp
QUEEN.

I'm a walking exclamation point!
And this QUEEN never disappoints.

Baby queen!
Yes, you down there!
If you're ever looking for a
silk pajama
melodrama
zero trauma
drag mama,
I'm your
QUEEN.

Just be warned:
once we let you in
the real show will begin.

The first night of their trip, Sam suggested they go to Finocchio's, a nightclub famous for its drag shows and female impersonators. "It was the craziest place," Evelyn said later. "Magic." Finocchio's hosted four shows a night starting at 9 p.m. and ending at 2 a.m., six days a week. The shows featured singers, dancers, comic acts, and celebrity impersonators. Often real celebrities were in the audience. It was a popular tourist attraction, and drag clubs like Finocchio's were one of the few places gay men could socialize in public.

After enjoying the show, the foursome walked back to the Fairmont Hotel where they were staying, then headed to the bar. At that point, the conversation turned more serious. Sam cut right to the chase and said, "Evelyn, it is your scientific duty to study people like us. We have let you see us as we are, and people don't know what we are really. It's your duty to study people like us."

"I couldn't do that," said Evelyn. "You are my friends. I couldn't be objective about you."

Sam wouldn't let go. "We'll get a whole new group. We can get as many as a hundred gay guys if you want."

Evelyn didn't commit one way or the other. But she couldn't shake the idea. Even after they returned to Los Angeles, Sam continued to pester her about it. But Evelyn had her doubts. Eventually, Evelyn sought the advice of her office mate at UCLA, Bruno Klopfer. "He's right," her colleague said. "We don't know anything about men like him, and he's absolutely right. You should do it."

Shortly afterwards, Evelyn started her research by conducting interviews and gathering information. She didn't have an organized game plan, though, and she knew that a major shortcoming to her research was the lack of a control group—a group of straight men she could compare her gay male participants to. What she didn't anticipate was that life would take another unexpected twist, and her research would come to a screeching halt.

Mercy

I drink too much. I'm
destroying myself. I don't
want to destroy you.[3]

The poem "Mercy" reflects exactly what Donn said to Evelyn one night in 1947. Donn was an alcoholic, and he could see how his addiction was affecting his marriage. When he announced that he wanted a divorce, Evelyn's world shattered. They'd been married for only six years, and now she found herself once again a single woman.

After the breakup of her marriage, Evelyn didn't want to stay in Los Angeles. She took a job at Bryn Mawr College outside of Philadelphia, Pennsylvania, thinking that she would remain there long-term. However, as the saying goes, "wherever you go, there you are." She couldn't stop thinking about Sam and George, her friends at the house on Benton Way, and the research she'd begun. By the end of her first year at Bryn Mawr, Evelyn decided to return to Los Angeles.

Evelyn didn't want to go back to the house she'd once shared with Donn, so she found a small guest-house in the Brentwood neighborhood of Los Angeles, not far from UCLA. The landlord, a man named Edward Hooker, agreed to rent it to her. An English professor at the university, Edward had recently been divorced, and Evelyn and Edward took a liking to one another. She began to spend time with him at the main house on the property, and they sometimes went out together. After a period of time, Edward invited Evelyn to join him on a trip to Cambria, a pretty coastal town north of Los Angeles. She agreed, never once thinking that Edward was at all attracted to her! Cambria quickly became one of her favorite places, and she remembered this trip throughout her life as one of the best experiences she ever had. By the end of that trip, she knew that she and Edward were in love with each other, and in 1951, Evelyn and Edward married.

The breakup of her relationship with Donn was undoubtedly painful for Evelyn, but she was able to put her life back together. Newly married to a man she loved dearly, Evelyn felt ready to get back to her research on gay men.[4]

"Homosexual attachments are not quite so common among men but they are frequent enough to be easily observed. Most of such attachments are mere passing phases of development, and the subjects of them go on to heterosexual relationships. When, however, some peculiar attitude exists toward the other sex one may persist in a homosexual attachment. These relationships should consequently not be regarded in too superficial a light. They are a danger sign."[5]

This passage, from a college psychology textbook published in 1928, is likely similar to what Evelyn might have read in her own textbooks—and, before meeting Sam From and his friends, what she might have taught to her students. It reflected the attitudes towards sexual orientations other than straight in the general public. People thought same-sex attraction and sexual behavior was either a phase or caused by poor parenting or inappropriate gender roles. While some urban areas enjoyed a thriving gay subculture, the general population viewed same-sex attraction and behavior with disdain and disgust.

However, what was written in the textbooks Evelyn read may not have reflected the opinions of all psychologists and doctors at the time. The English doctor Havelock Ellis, for example, didn't consider same-sex attraction to be a crime, a disorder, or an immoral perversion. His book *Sexual Inversion*, published in 1896, was the first medical textbook about same-sex attraction and sexual behavior, and was the first published source of objective data on the topic.

Meanwhile, in Germany during that same time period, a German doctor named Magnus Hirschfeld established the Scientific Humanitarian Committee, which was organized to advocate for the rights of gay people and overturn Paragraph 175, the section of the German penal code that criminalized what was termed "unnatural sexual offenses" between men. In 1917, Hirschfeld published a book titled *The Homosexuality of Men and Women*, and two years later he opened the Institute for Sexual Research in Berlin. Both Ellis and Hirschfeld were also among the first to write about and study the experience of being a person who is transgender.

Sigmund Freud's theories also powerfully impacted the public. Freud had popularized the idea of the Oedipus complex—the idea that young boys, jealous of their fathers, harbor an unconscious desire to kill their fathers so they can have their mothers' attention all to themselves. How boys resolve this conflict, according to Freud, plays a strong role in determining sexual orientation. It sounds completely absurd, but this theory quickly gained traction, and soon became the dominant perspective. Neo-Freudian theories of the 1950s took this theory a step further—if boys were too close to their mothers and didn't absorb enough masculine energy from their fathers, they'd become too soft and feminine, and they'd probably end up being gay.

Although Freud's theories have been weaponized against the gay community, they didn't tell the entire story. While Freud believed that same-sex attraction and sexual behavior wasn't the typical developmental path, he didn't believe that it was a disorder. At least two pieces of evidence point to this. First, we know that in 1930, Freud had signed a petition opposing the criminalization and treatment of "homosexuality." Second, we have Freud's now-famous "Letter to an American Mother." In 1935, Freud responded to a letter he'd received from a woman, who'd reached out to the famous psychoanalyst because she'd recently learned her son was gay (although she couldn't bring herself to say it outright). She was very distressed by the news, and wanted to know whether or not his "condition" could be successfully treated. Freud responded by saying that being gay is not an illness, and that her son should not be subjected to any form of treatment to try to change his sexual orientation. A portion of Freud's response is quoted in the poem "Freud."

Unfortunately, none of these perspectives made an immediate difference. Two notable events occurred in 1935, the year Freud penned his letter. A professor at New York University named Louis Max presented a paper at the American Psychological Association conference titled "Breaking Up a Homosexual Fixation by the Conditional Reaction Technique." This presentation was the first documented use of aversive conditioning—otherwise known as electric shock therapy—to treat "homosexuality." The poem "Shocker" contains the original language from Dr. Max's presentation.

The other event that occurred in 1935 was Magnus Hirschfield's death from a heart attack. He had been living in exile in France ever since a Nazi-led mass book-burning two years earlier, which destroyed much of the archives of his Institute for Sexual Research in Berlin. His research was gone, and now so was he.

Shocker

Low shock intensities
had little effect
but intensities
considerably
higher
than those
usually employed
on
human
subjects
in other studies
definitely
diminished
the emotional value
of the stimulus
for
days
after each
experimental
period.[6]

. Freud's letter was published in the *American Journal of Psychiatry* in 1951. One year later, the first edition of the American Psychiatric Association's Diagnostic and Statistical Manual of Mental Disorders (also known as the DSM) classified "homosexuality" as a mental disorder. The DSM is widely regarded as the main source for classifying and defining all mental health disorders; an updated edition is still used today, but the classification of "homosexuality" as a disorder has since been removed.

Freud

Homosexuality is assuredly no advantage,
but it is nothing to be ashamed of,
no vice, no degradation,
it cannot be classified as an illness;
we consider it to be a variation
of the sexual function
produced by a certain arrest
of sexual development.
Many highly respectable individuals
of ancient and modern times
have been homosexuals,
several of the greatest men
among them
(Plato,
Michelangelo,
Leonardo da Vinci, etc.).
It is a great injustice
to persecute homosexuality
as a crime and cruelty too.

Chapter 3

Stranger Danger

Don't take candy from strangers.

Never tell a stranger your name or address.

Don't get into a car with someone you don't know.

Children often get this kind of advice in school. Although "stranger danger" crimes against children are relatively infrequent (it's far more likely for children to be harmed by someone they know), it does happen, and it's good for children to know what to do. However, sometimes this advice can be taken too far, and used inappropriately. That was certainly the case during the post-World War II era, when "stranger danger" was associated with the unfounded idea of "homosexual predators."

The poem "The Case of Jimmy" comes directly from the script of a 1961 short film called "Boys

Beware." The film warns children about the dangers of men who might attempt to lure young boys into sexually inappropriate situations. Four cases are presented in the film: "Jimmy," who is lured into a friendship with a stranger and becomes the victim of sexually inappropriate behavior; "Mike," who accepts a ride from a stranger and is presumably killed by him; "Denny," whose friends spot him entering a stranger's car and alert his mother to the danger; and "Bobby," who is followed into a public restroom by a stranger. All of the strangers in the film are portrayed as gay men, and same-sex attraction and sexual behavior is repeatedly described as a sickness or a disease.

Films like this, called "social guidance films," were frequently shown in elementary schools throughout the United States. Filmed in a suburb of Los Angeles, just a few miles from Evelyn's home and the UCLA campus, "Boys Beware" promoted the widely-held notion that same-sex attraction and sexual behavior was a mental disorder, and that gay men were dangerous predators in need of treatment.

The Case of Jimmy

What Jimmy didn't know
was that Ralph was sick.
A sickness that was not visible
like smallpox
but no less dangerous and contagious.
A sickness of the mind.
You see, Ralph was a homosexual.
A person who demands an intimate
relationship with members
of their own
sex.

This poem comes directly from the script of
The Case of Jimmy.

Treatment Plan

Aversive conditioning
Bladder washing
Castration
Drowning drugs
Exorcism
Father figures
Group therapy
Hypnosis
Ice water immersion
Journaling
Klonopin
Lobotomy
Masculinity training
Nothing works
Orgone therapy
Prayer
Quaker Oats
Rectal massage
Shock treatments
Testosterone injections
Uterine surgeries
Vomiting
Womb calming
Xanax
Yin yang therapy
Zen Buddhism

All of the "treatments" listed in the poem "Treatment Plan" were actually used to try to "cure" people of their "homosexuality." Before drug therapies were available, psychiatric patients were subjected to a wide range of strange, barbaric, and ineffective treatments. Hydrotherapy was one form of treatment commonly used in the 19th and early 20th centuries. Patients were immersed in ice water for hours or even days, swaddled in ice-cold towels, and strapped to the wall and sprayed with a powerful hose. Another bizarre therapeutic approach was the practice of eating bland foods, like cornflakes or oatmeal, to curb sexual impulses. Dr. John Harvey Kellogg, the creator of Kellogg's Cornflakes, was a major advocate of this approach.

One of the more barbaric approaches of the 19th century involved using wide metal coils to deliver electric shocks to the body. By the mid-20th century, these electric shock therapies became more sophisticated. Electroconvulsive therapy (ECT), which rose in popularity during the 1940s and 1950s, involved delivering electric shocks directly to the brain to induce a grand mal seizure. Aversive conditioning, another form of electric shock treatment, required patients to receive powerful electric shocks while looking at same-sex images that gay people could possibly find attractive.

When nothing else worked, surgeries were often used as a last resort. Some of them included sexual surgeries like hysterectomies and castrations; bladder washing, in which a catheter was inserted to flush out the bladder; and rectal massage, which involved a doctor inserting a small device into the rectum to massage the prostate.[7]

When psychotropic drugs became more widely available, they either replaced earlier practices (like hydrotherapy) or accompanied those treatments (like electric shock therapy). People who were institutionalized because of their same-sex desires were routinely given a cocktail of antidepressants, anti-anxiety drugs, and/or antipsychotic medications. These medications had numerous side effects, some of which were permanent and debilitating. In addition, patients were often given drugs that either increased or blocked the production of sex hormones, drugs that induced vomiting, or drugs that made people feel like they were drowning, in an effort to curb them of their desires.

Not all gay people were institutionalized, and not all were in some form of therapy to "cure" them. Home-grown approaches were (and still are, unfortunately) quite common. Parents were encouraged to punish boys for playing with dolls or doing other girly things and reward them for playing sports.

Girls who seemed tomboyish were encouraged to wear dresses, jewelry, and makeup. Both of these responses are addressing gender expression, which we know now may have nothing to do with a person's future sexual orientation. Child-rearing books stressed the importance of a strong father figure in the household, presumably to push masculine gender roles and straight orientation. Teenagers were encouraged to date people of the opposite sex, and adults were pressured to get married as a way of curing their same-sex attractions.

The late 20th century and early 21st century saw the rise of using religion to treat or prevent unaccepted sexual orientations. Some ministries based in fundamentalist Christianity have relied on prayer, masculinity training, Bible studies, and outright shaming. Other religions have been invoked as well: using Zen Buddhist meditation practices to curb sexual impulses; using Eastern religions like Taoism to achieve a balance between "yin" (feminine) and "yang" (masculine) energy; or, in a more extreme approach, performing an exorcism, a traditional Catholic rite used to cast out demons.

Treatments like these were widespread when Evelyn Hooker was conducting her research. None of it worked, and most of it was traumatizing and damaging.

Six Minutes

it took only six minutes
after the earthquake rattled his body
don't blink, said the doctor
crying wasn't an option

after the earthquake rattled his body
the doctor raised the ice pick
crying wasn't an option
insert, tap, twist, remove

the doctor raised the ice pick
eyes wide open
insert, tap, twist, remove
his soul screamed silently

eyes wide open
tornado ripping through
his soul screamed silently
on to the next one

tornado ripping through
lights out
on to the next one
it only took six minutes

lights out
goodnight sleep tight
it only took six minutes
he was still gay

The poem "Six Minutes" describes the experience of undergoing a transorbital lobotomy, a procedure that was frequently used to treat same-sex attractions. Lobotomies are an ugly chapter in psychiatric history. The first lobotomies, performed in 1935 by Portuguese neurologists Dr. Antonio Egas Moniz and Dr. Almeida Lima, involved drilling holes directly into the skull. However, this procedure was very dangerous, often resulting in permanent damage to other parts of the brain. An American neurologist and psychiatrist named Dr. Walter Freeman, who had been performing lobotomies since 1936, wanted to find a way to perform lobotomies more quickly and efficiently, and without drilling holes into the skull. The best way to do that, Freeman reasoned, was to access the brain through the patient's eye sockets.

Here's how it worked: Before starting the procedure, Freeman sedated the patient by administering electroconvulsive shock. He then inserted a tool that resembled an ice pick (leading to the term "ice pick lobotomy") through the top of the eye socket, tapping lightly on the pick with a hammer. After twisting it to cut through the brain's neural fibers, the pick was removed, and the procedure was repeated on the other side. In total, the transorbital lobotomy took about six minutes to perform.

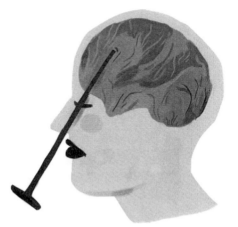

This new method made it much easier for a patient to get this procedure. For $25, you could get a transorbital lobotomy, and you could be home in less than an hour.[8] Freeman traveled throughout the United States to perform transorbital lobotomies in mental hospitals, and he also taught doctors and non-surgeons how to do them. In the United States, about 50,000 patients were lobotomized, most of them between the late 1940s and mid-1950s. Dr. Freeman performed between 3,500 and 5,000 of those lobotomies, 40% of which were on gay patients.[9]

Did it work? As many as 15% of those who had been lobotomized died, and many more patients were severely impaired as a result of the procedure, greatly out-weighing the number of people who reported positive outcomes.

Secrecy

CONCLUSION

███ The ███

██

██

████ Government ████████████████████████████████

█████████████████████████████ is █████████████████

██

██

████ on ███

██

███████████████████████ alert ████████████████████

PERVERTS CALLED "GOVERNMENT PERIL";

PURGE OF SEX PERVERTS IN U.S. JOBS IS PUSHED;

126 HOMOSEXUALS FIRED BY STATE DEPARTMENT

These were the breaking news headlines of 1950. Anti-gay attitudes had ramped up considerably after World War II. They saturated the media. They were part of the public school curriculum. And they were widely held by psychologists, psychiatrists, and doctors. By 1950, the U.S. government had also jumped onto the anti-gay bandwagon. They claimed that same-sex attraction was associated with communists, and therefore were a threat to the security of the American people.

It's troubling to think about how the government made this connection—especially since research was just starting to emerge that contradicted stereotypes about gay people. Alfred Kinsey's groundbreaking 1948 study is a good example. Titled *Sexual Behavior in the Human Male*, Kinsey's study revealed that sexual orientations other than straight were more common than people had previously thought. Approximately 10% of the 5,300 men he studied were gay, and nearly 50% had had some sexual experience with another man. Kinsey didn't believe that same-sex attraction was a disorder or a crime, and the fact that it was so common seemed to suggest that it was a different kind of "normal."

Kinsey's report was a victim of bad timing. In 1948, the same year his study was published, Congress passed a law "to provide for the treatment of sexual psychopaths in the District of Columbia"— including gay people. If someone was caught engaging in same-sex sexual behavior, they could be arrested, labeled as mentally ill, and fined up to $1,000 or sentenced to up to 10 years in prison.[10] This law set a new precedent for the persecution of gay men. In addition, the release of Kinsey's study made people realize how common being gay is, leading them to think: *The person next door could be gay!* While eventually Kinsey's study contributed to the growing acceptance of lesbian, gay, bisexual, and trans people, initially it did the exact opposite— stoking fears that gay people were dangerous and were infiltrating society.

This fear started when, in 1950, U.S. Senator Joseph McCarthy kicked off a national "Red Scare" with a speech claiming that he had a list of more than 200 government employees who were "known communists." It didn't take long for government officials to suggest gay people were communists, creating a spinoff "Lavender Scare." Two weeks after he gave his speech, Senator McCarthy presented specific case examples to the U.S. Senate of communists who were employed by the government. Two of these cases—Case #14 and Case #62—involved gay men. A week after that, Deputy Undersecretary of State John Peurifoy announced that 91 gay men who were government employees had been fired.

Investigations of suspected communists (and gay people) in the government kicked into high gear. A Senate subcommittee conducted an investigation between March and May of 1950, claiming that more than 3,000 gay people worked for the U.S. government. On June 7, 1950, in response to this subcommittee's report, Congress approved a resolution to conduct a more thorough investigation of "the alleged employment by the departments and agencies of the Government of homosexuals and other moral perverts."

This investigation took place during the remainder of the year, and in December 1950, the committee issued a report titled *Employment of Homosexuals and Other Sex Perverts in Government*. The report concluded that gay people should not be employed by the federal government because they were "generally unsuitable" and constituted "security risks." The report also concluded that "homosexuality" was a sexual perversion that was dangerous to young people, and that gay people were immoral and emotionally unstable. Even though the committee had heard testimony from doctors and other experts that being gay is not immoral, criminal, or unhealthy, they ignored it. "One homosexual," the report warned, "can pollute a Government office."[11]

This document (also known as the Hoey report, named for Senator Clyde Hoey, who led the committee) ultimately led to a complete ban on gay people in government jobs. In 1953, President Dwight D. Eisenhower signed Executive Order 10450, which established security requirements for people who wanted to work for the U.S. government. Because gay people were automatically viewed as a security threat, this Executive Order prevented them from getting a government job.

What does all of this have to do with Evelyn Hooker's study? If she was going to do her study, she needed money. In 1953—the same year President Eisenhower signed Executive Order 10450—Evelyn applied for a grant from the National Institute of Mental Health (NIMH), a federal government agency, to fund her study. It was a bold move on Evelyn's part to ask the U.S. government to give her money to study "homosexuality"—especially since she wanted to prove that it was just as normal as other "normal" sexual orientations. The likelihood of the NIMH funding her study was low. The worst-case scenario? The government might think Evelyn's research interest was a "security risk." Even though

Evelyn didn't work for the government, she could still be blacklisted (as she had been previously when she tried to return to her job at Whittier College). She could lose her job and her reputation could be ruined.

The people at NIMH were caught off-guard by Evelyn's application. Usually, when people applied for research grants, they received a phone call or a letter informing them whether or not they will be awarded the money. Evelyn got an in-person visit from the chief of the grants division, John Eberhart. *Who was this woman?* he wondered. How could she possibly be connected to so many "normal" gay men—none of whom had ever been in prison or in a psychiatric ward? They spent the day together and had a pleasant visit. At the end of the day, Eberhart said to Evelyn: "We're prepared to make you the grant, but you may not receive it. Everyone is being investigated. If you don't receive it, you won't know why and we won't know why." Evelyn did, in fact, receive the grant, which was a miracle given the pervasiveness of the Red Scare.

Chapter 4

The Fairy Project

"We can get a hundred gay guys if you want."

That was what Sam From said to Evelyn the night he asked her to study gay men. And with the help of the local chapter of the Mattachine Society, one of the first gay rights organizations, he delivered on that promise. It helped that Evelyn had become an honorary member of the "club," and gay men in the Los Angeles area knew about her and trusted her. Finding 30 gay men to participate in her study was a relatively easy task, and Evelyn accomplished it quickly. As a researcher, Evelyn was in a class by herself, for no other straight psychologist would have been able to locate and convince a group of gay men to take part in a research study—especially given the repressive political and social attitudes towards sexual and gender minorities. Most gay men at the time were deeply in the closet, fearful of revealing their identities to others. The gay men who participated knew that Evelyn would hold their involvement in the strictest of confidences.

Finding straight men who were willing to participate was another story. It was widely believed that you could become gay just by being around gay people—or, for that matter, anything that *seemed* gay (like Evelyn's study). Word got around the UCLA campus about "the fairy project," (Eberhart later told Evelyn that this was what the grants committee called her study) and straight men wanted nothing to do with it. The fear of turning gay (or even being perceived as gay) kept straight men far, far away from Evelyn's study.

Evelyn had a solution: instead of conducting the research on the university's campus, she decided to have research participants come to the guest house on her property. The tiny house was separate from the main house, and the grounds of the property were spacious and private. "Once a person opened the garden gate," Evelyn recounted later, "he was invisible to the neighbors. Without this superb place

Slur

You know what it's called
back at the ranch? They call it
the Fairy Project.

in which to conduct the research, I would never have attempted it."[12]

Officials at the university had other ideas, though. They insisted that Evelyn conduct her research at the UCLA campus. In their minds, Evelyn was crossing a line by suggesting that research participants go to her home—and with any other study, Evelyn would have agreed. However, Evelyn knew that confidentiality, while critical in any research study, was especially important in this project. If the identities of her gay participants were revealed, they could be fired from their jobs, kicked out of their homes, committed to a mental institution, or thrown in jail. If her straight participants were identified and associated with this study, they risked a different kind of humiliation. Ultimately, the officials at UCLA relented, and allowed Evelyn to conduct her research at her estate.

Even with these protections, Evelyn still had trouble convincing straight men to participate. She eventually got desperate enough that she literally grabbed men off the street. Whenever a maintenance worker, police officer, or salesperson came to her home, Evelyn buttonholed them into participating in her research. "No man is safe on Saltair Avenue," her husband joked. Eventually, Evelyn was able to secure 30 straight male participants.

The Shack

he followed the path towards the shack
smelling blooms along the way
constantly watching his back

he scattered dirt over his tracks
feeling like a lion's prey
he followed the path towards the shack

he pictured himself turning back
sweating from the orange rays
constantly watching his back

he felt his resolve start to crack
the voice inside said run away
he followed the path towards the shack

he watched the door open a crack
she promised it would be okay
constantly watching his back

he knew he would never come back
but he would do this for today
he followed the path towards the shack
constantly watching his back

Imaging lying outside in a field, looking up at the clouds in the sky. What do they look like? An angel, perhaps, or a dragon, or a wolf? An angry face baring its teeth at you? A snow-capped mountain, or waves crashing on the sand?

But what are they really? *They're clouds.* Any meaning you might have assigned to those clouds came entirely from your imagination. And different people might see different things. One person might see a tiger's face, and another person looking at the same exact cloud might see two people kissing.

Back in the 1950s, most of the psychological tests used to identify personality traits and psychological issues were, quite simply, versions of the cloud game. These projective tests involved asking people to respond to some kind of vague, ambiguous stimulus. For example, you might be given an image of an ink-blot and asked to describe what that inkblot might be. Or you might be given a blank piece of paper and be asked to draw a picture of a house. Or you might be handed an image of a boy sitting at a table looking at a violin and be asked to tell a story about what you see. The objects you see in the inkblot, the way you draw the house, the story you choose to tell about the picture—all of those things are thought to reveal something about who you are. Because only you can

Inkblot Test

bat   moth

wolf   fox

alien   angel

ribcage   uterus

battleship   spaceship

ballet dancer   squashed bug

exploding mushroom cloud   out-of-control whirling dervish

two birds at a bird feeder the Virgin Mary surrounded by angels two women dancing

a battleship that got shot at a woman with her head chopped off two pigs attacking an angel

an animal standing at the edge of a pond staring at its reflection

character in a horror film   a damaged heart   a lonely abandoned dog

a nightmare that won't end   butterfly   a person praying for help

when will this test be over when will this test be over when will this test be over

a lighted Jack o'Lantern the devil waiting for me in hell four candy corns

two tiny hands reaching up   the Titanic sinking   two lips yearning for a kiss

a man flexing his muscles   oh no oh no oh no   a man flexing his muscles

is that enough responses for you

how on earth can a bunch of cards

with ink splattered on them

tell you that

I'm

gay?

see what you see, or draw what you draw, or tell the stories you tell.

All of these tests, particularly the Rorschach, were commonly used in the 1950s by psychologists to "diagnose" someone with "homosexuality." Evelyn questioned whether they actually did so accurately, and this study provided an opportunity to test that hypothesis. Each person who participated took three projective tests. The first was the Rorschach, a test consisting of 10 cards with inkblots printed on them. The second test was called the Thematic Apperception Test (TAT), which involved viewing a series of images and telling a story inspired by the image. The third test was called the Make A Picture Story Test (MAPS). Similar to the TAT, the MAPS consisted of a series of background pictures—a living room, a street, a bridge, and so on—together with a collection of human and animal cutout figures. Participants were asked to arrange one or more of the figures on a background and then tell a story about the resulting picture.

Thirty gay male and thirty straight male participants completed each test. After scoring them herself, Evelyn asked three additional psychologists—all of whom were experts at the interpretation of projective tests—to review the test protocols. The first was Bruno Klopfer, her office mate at UCLA—and the person who, years earlier, had encouraged Evelyn to go through with her study. Dr. Klopfer knew the Rorschach better than anyone in the world, making him the perfect choice. The second was Mortimer Meyer, a psychologist at the Veterans Administration clinic and an expert in both the Rorschach and the TAT. The team of experts was rounded out by the creator of the MAPS test, Edwin Shneidman. Dr. Shneidman, who was also an expert on the study of suicide, was drawn to this study in part because of the number of gay people who took their own lives.

The experts were given two tasks: to assign a rating of each individual's overall psychological adjustment, using a scale from one (superior) to five (maladjusted); and to determine, using the information from the projective tests, whether each participant was straight or gay. For the psychological adjustment portion, on all three tests, two-thirds of the research participants in each group were assigned a rating of three (average) or better. Put another way, there was no measurable difference between straight men and gay men in their overall psychological adjustment.

The experts felt more confident about their second task. Shneidman, in particular, was positive he'd be able to identify who was gay and who was straight. "If you showed me the protocols for 30 schizophrenics," he said, using the psychotic disorder as a comparison, "I'd be surprised if I didn't get 28." His hit rate for this was no better than the flip of a coin. Surprised and a little irritated by the results, Shneidman asked for another chance to review the test protocols. He was no more successful the second time. Other than a few instances where gay participants revealed their sexual orientation in their TAT and MAPS stories, it was impossible for the experts to correctly identify a person's sexual orientation using these tests.

There was only one conclusion the judges could reach: "[H]omosexuality is not a diagnostic category."[13]

Evelyn included several case examples to illustrate the range of personalities and levels of adjustment her gay participants exhibited. Not all of the participants were psychologically healthy, and at least one was downright unstable. However, the majority of them were quite well-adjusted, exhibiting the wide range of personality characteristics that makes each of us unique. The following "found poems" consist of direct quotes from the experts who evaluated the test protocols. In both examples, each individual was judged to be healthy, and both were incorrectly identified as a straight man. Prior to reviewing Man #16's MAPS test, Shneidman had no doubt in his mind that the person he was evaluating was a straight man. When Shneidman saw that Man #16 had revealed he was a gay man during his MAPS test (he selected two male figures and placed them on a bed together, then told a story about them), Shneidman was shocked, then humbled. "He is the most heterosexual looking homosexual I have ever seen," he concluded.

Man #16

Sensitive.
Responsive.
Ethical.
Balanced on a razor's edge.
Gives an original twist
to ordinary things.
For him it is very important
not to be conventional.
He avoids it like the plague.
He tries to keep it cool.
I think he is heterosexual.
The most heterosexual looking homosexual
I have ever seen.

Man #50

So ordinary.
It's hard to say anything
specific
about him.
He must be a heterosexual.
I would really have to
force
myself
to think of him
as not
heterosexual.
A solid citizen,
neatly and solidly
integrated.

In her paper titled "The Adjustment of the Male Overt Homosexual," published in 1957 in the *Journal of Projective Techniques*, Evelyn offered the following research conclusions:

1. Homosexuality as a clinical entity does not exist. Its forms are as varied as are those of heterosexuality.

2. Homosexuality may be a deviation in sexual pattern which is within the normal range. This has been suggested, on a biological level, by Ford and Beach.

3. The role of particular forms of sexual desire and expression in personality structure and development may be less important than has frequently been assumed. Even if one assumes that homosexuality represents a severe form of maladjustment to society in the sexual sector of behavior, this does not necessarily mean that the homosexual must be severely maladjusted in other sectors of his behavior. Or, if one assumes that homosexuality is a form of severe

maladjustment internally, it may be that the disturbance is limited to the sexual sector alone.

In a nutshell, what Evelyn was saying was this:

1. Homosexuality is not a disorder.

2. Homosexuality is one of many forms of normal sexual expression.

3. While some homosexual people may experience psychological difficulties, homosexual people as a group are not poorly adjusted.

These were bold and radical assertions, especially in 1957.

٭

Shortly after Evelyn completed her study, two tragic and unexpected events occurred. In 1956, Sam From, who had been vacationing at the trendy Salton Sea resort area, died in a car accident on his way home. "He was always a very generous person," Evelyn said later. "All his friends, myself included, were absolutely devastated."[14] Sam's death happened right before Evelyn was scheduled to present the results of her study at the American Psychological Association convention in Chicago.

A few months later, in January of 1957, Evelyn was in Palm Springs vacationing with friends when she received even more devastating news. Her husband, Edward Hooker, had died unexpectedly of a heart attack.[15] The sudden loss deeply shook her, and she grieved her beloved husband for the rest of her life. However, she didn't repeat what she did after her first marriage broke up—this time she stayed in Los Angeles, continued her work, and leaned on her friends and colleagues for support. Her study was published in the *Journal of Projective Techniques* later that same year.

Elegy

Oh, my loves! Can you hear me from within
those awful crypts entrapping you herein?
Your heart, so full and teeming with passion,
exploding, shot by Death's cruel assassin.
Your clever mind so full of potential,
a fiery crash wrecking your soul so gentle.
My tattered soul, worn threadbare without you.
Oh, Death! So callous, brutal, cold-blooded
knifing my heart, leaving me drawn and gutted.
And yet, I make a promise to you both.
To my work I am forever betrothed.
Your steadfast faith in me made me complete.
I pledge to you I will never retreat.

Chapter 5

Backlash

By the end of the 1950s, the television had become a solid member of the average American family. More than two-thirds of American households owned a television, and that number increased every year. *TV Guide* was the bestselling magazine of the late 1950s. Families sat in their living rooms and ate TV dinners on their metal tray tables. They watched shows depicting television's idea of the "perfect family"—a breadwinner father, briefcase in hand, who headed off to work each day, and a loving, pearl-studded housewife in an A-line dress who chuckled every time her rambunctious sons were up to mischief. Or they watched variety shows like *The Ed Sullivan*

Show, American Bandstand, or *The Lawrence Welk Show.* Westerns, where the good guys always triumphed over the bad guys, were also popular. And then there were rural comedies, like *The Beverly Hillbillies* and *The Andy Griffith Show,* which poked fun at small-town country life. These were considered to be "wholesome" family viewing, suitable for all ages.

Because people could also watch the news on TV, they could get up-to-the-minute, breaking news in real time. Ironically, what they saw on the news was far different from what they watched on scheduled television programs. TV shows featured traditional White middle-class families dealing with comical daily life issues. Real life, in contrast, looked far different. People were still terrified of communists. Racial tensions were brewing, with White families fleeing racially diverse urban areas for the suburbs. And the persecution of gay people was in full swing.

᛫ᛡ᛫

On the night of March 7, 1967, those two worlds came together. Families who were watching television that night were treated to an episode of *Petticoat Junction,* set in rural America at the Shady Rest Hotel. There was Kate, the owner of the hotel; her Uncle

Joe, and sisters Billie Jo, Bobbie Jo, and Betty Jo. Each episode was a comedy-filled half-hour, with corny jokes, goofy hijinks, and silly misunderstandings— sprinkled with good old-fashioned gender stereotypes. Every night, the show always ended with a clear resolution, like a tidy bow on a birthday gift. Good, clean fun for the whole family.

If families didn't turn off the television right after *Petticoat Junction* ended, they would have been in for a shock. A special episode of *CBS Television Reports* aired that night. It was called "The Homosexuals,"

and it was narrated by Mike Wallace, who went on to become a correspondent for the popular show *60 Minutes*. This marked the first time the topic of same-sex attraction was discussed openly on a network television station.

The documentary started off with this statement: "Most Americans are repelled by the mere notion of homosexuality," reported Wallace in the documentary. "A CBS poll shows two out of three Americans look on homosexuality with disgust, discomfort, or fear." That quote set the tone for the entire documentary, and made clear that same sex-attraction wasn't going to be portrayed as normal or healthy.

The film went on to feature interviews with three gay men. Although two of them were quite comfortable with their sexuality, the third man who was interviewed was the most memorable. Filmed in shadow behind a potted plant in order to conceal his identity, he was described by Wallace as a 27-year-old college-educated man who was unable to hold a job "because of his inability to contain his homosexual inclinations." Wallace added: "He's been in jail three times for committing homosexual acts. If he is arrested once more, he faces the possibility of life in prison. He is now on probation and in psychotherapy."

Quality Family Time

Every Tuesday night
we watched Petticoat Junction.
A wholesome show
you could watch with your children.

Every episode was filled with bad jokes,
chicken and dumplings,
a laugh track,
and the same exact plot line.

One night
we kept watching after the credits rolled
and we saw something
that wasn't so wholesome.

They turned off the TV.

Next, the film featured two "experts." Dr. Charles Socarides and Dr. Irving Bieber were what were known as "neo-Freudians," taking Sigmund Freud's original theories and modifying them to apply to social and cultural issues. Both of them believed that same-sex attraction was caused by a suffocating, domineering mother and an absent father. They also believed that it was a disorder that could be cured. Bieber, in particular, claimed that one-third of the patients he'd treated for same-sex attraction and sexual behavior were successful in becoming straight. Interestingly, despite the fact that many psychologists and psychiatrists (including Evelyn Hooker) believed that same-sex attraction was not a disorder, the program failed to include any of them. Viewers were left with the impression that these two men represented the entire mental health professional community.

Mike Wallace's final words in "The Homosexuals" are depicted in the found poem "Lies."

*

It was radical for a network television station to air a show about this topic. Advertisers wouldn't buy commercial spots because of the subject matter, so CBS aired public service announcements instead.

Lies

The dilemma of the homosexual:
told by the medical profession he is sick;
by the law that he's a criminal;
shunned by employers;
rejected by heterosexual society;
incapable of a fulfilling relationship
with a woman,
or for that matter,
with a man.
At the center of his life
he remains
anonymous.
A displaced person.
An outsider.

Unfortunately, it also contributed to the cultural brainwashing that was already occurring throughout the US, cementing even further in the public's minds that same-sex attraction was a dangerous sickness that needed to be treated.

In the film, Bieber said, "Most mothers were involved in an unusually close and over-intimate relationship with their son. He was generally their favorite. She spent a great deal of time with him, and often mothers openly preferred their sons to their husbands. Although themselves rather puritanical and portraying for the son a concept of maleness and masculinity as brutish and animal-like, they were frequently seductive, and engaged in inappropriate bathroom and sleeping arrangements with their sons."

Bieber had earlier made a name for himself by attempting to "cure" patients of their same-sex attractions. In his 1962 study, titled *Homosexuality: A Psychoanalytic Study of Male Homosexuals*, Bieber outlined his theory that overinvolved mothers were the root cause of the issue. The solution? A strong, masculine father figure. "I do not believe that it is possible to produce a homosexual if the father is a warm, good, supportive, constructive father to his son," Bieber also said in the film.

Bieber's study was a counter-reaction to Kinsey's research, and it got considerably more attention than Evelyn's research did—despite the fact that Bieber's study had at least one fatal flaw. For starters, Bieber studied men who were already in therapy, whereas Evelyn studied men in the general population who hadn't necessarily received therapy. It's like studying the prevalence of alcoholism in society by recruiting participants at a bar.

Despite that serious bias, Bieber's research was widely reported on in the media, fueling negative stereotypes in the minds of the public. One example: the June 26, 1964 issue of *LIFE* magazine featured two articles about the topic, opening with a stereotypical description of gay men: "These brawny young men in their leather caps, shirts, jackets and pants are practicing homosexuals, men who turn to other men for affection and sexual satisfaction. They are part of what they call the 'gay world,' which is actually a sad and often sordid world." After asserting that gay men are now "discarding their furtive ways and openly admitting, even flaunting, their deviation," the article contends that "[t]his social disorder, which society tries to suppress, has forced itself into the public eye because it does present a problem—and parents especially are concerned."[16]

A Limerick for Dr. Bieber

There once was a doctor named Irving
whose theories were rather unnerving.
It seems so cliché
that moms make their sons gay!
A theory that's not worth preserving.

The second article in that *LIFE* magazine issue, titled "Scientists search for answers to a touchy and puzzling question: Why?" devotes six lengthy paragraphs to Bieber's research. Evelyn Hooker's work, in contrast, got three sentences.

Bieber wasn't the only one influencing the attitudes of the American public towards gay men. Socarides, who also appeared in *The Homosexuals*, advocated the idea that same-sex attraction, while a disorder, could be treated and ultimately cured. His work paved the way for therapists to offer "reparative therapy" to help gay men become straight. The importance of a "strong father figure" in a young boy's life, one of the central concepts in his 1968 book, *The Overt Homosexual*, grabbed hold of the general public. It became common belief that fatherless families were the root of all evil—and could turn little boys gay. But the ray of hope Bieber and Socarides offered was this: at least this sickness was treatable.

In the mainstream culture, Evelyn's work was barely a whisper. But by the late 1960s, gay and lesbian activism was heating up—and Evelyn's work spoke loudly and clearly to them. They knew that her research could be a powerful tool, and they were ready to use it.

A Limerick for Dr. Socarides

There once was a doctor named Charles
who believed same-sex love was immoral.
He realized his worst fear
when his son said, "I'm queer."
He could no longer rest on his laurels.

While Bieber and Socarides were getting airtime in the media, Evelyn was steadily making an impact in her own way. In 1961, Evelyn received an NIMH Research Career Award, which gave her funding to help her continue her research. That same year, she was invited to lecture about her research in Europe. Both of these opportunities helped her share her findings with a wider audience. But the big break happened in 1967, when Stanley Yolles, the director of the NIMH, contacted Evelyn to tell her about a special task force he wanted to convene. Yolles wanted the task force to come up with recommendations for the NIMH regarding what to do about same-sex attractions and sexual behaviors. Should the NIMH recommend specific treatments for or "cures"? Should gay people be put in jail and punished for their behavior? Or should the NIMH reject the idea that this is a disorder?

The task force, Yolles said, would include a variety of people—psychologists, psychiatrists, legal and law enforcement experts, religious scholars. He wanted Evelyn to chair the task force. Evelyn said yes.

Two years later, under Evelyn's leadership, the Task Force completed their report and submitted it to the NIMH. Their recommendations included the following:

Hope

You hoped that this process would work out as planned.
You hoped that the doctors would keep their mouths shut.
You hoped that the lawyers would side with the cops.
You hoped that the preachers would sway the report.
You hoped they would say we were mentally ill.
You hoped they would tell you how we could be cured.
You hoped they'd say how to make us go away.
You hoped they'd give parents some useful advice.
You hoped it would quietly sink out of sight.
You hoped that you wouldn't get canned from your job.
You hoped we'd forget all about the whole thing.

We hoped you were seriously going to help.
We hoped that you really weren't kidding this time.
We hoped you would tell them that we were okay.
We hoped that our families would listen to you.
We hoped we'd survive all the shocks and the drugs.
We hoped the police raids would start to die down.
We hoped you'd release us from those padded rooms.
We hoped you would loosen the shackles and cuffs.
We hoped you'd prevent them from laying us off.
We hoped you'd protect us from getting beat up.
We hoped that you wouldn't betray us again.
We hope that you learn from your vile mistakes.

1. Create a Center for the Study of
    Sexuality, where scientists could study
    a range of issues pertaining to homosex-
    uality (and other sexuality topics). This
    center could also be a training hub to
    help mental health professionals, police
    officers, educators, and members of the
    public better understand homosexuality.

2. Shift treatment efforts away from trying
    to change a person's sexual orientation,
    and instead focus on helping people be
    happy and well-adjusted.

3. Make changes in laws and in employ-
    ment practices. More specifically, the
    task force recommended repealing laws
    and policies that discriminate against
    homosexual people, specifically laws
    that criminalize homosexuality.

These recommendations were simple, yet bold. No
one had ever stated in a public government document the idea that same-sex attractions and sexual
behaviors should be decriminalized—let alone
declassified as a disorder. Since Yolles was the person
who appointed Evelyn to be the chair, he must have

known on some level that the task force recommendations would represent a shift in thinking and in practice. Evelyn was well known for being an ally to the gay community, and as the chair, her perspective would be a strong influence on the task force. But all of the recommendations were approved by a strong majority of the group, and most were approved unanimously.

Yet the NIMH wasn't ready to be bold. The report was submitted to the NIMH just before Richard M. Nixon was elected President of the United States. Nixon was a staunch anti-Communist, and likely would not be supportive of the task force's recommendations. The top officials at NIMH decided to delay the publication of the report.

Meanwhile, the gay activist community in Los Angeles decided to take matters into their own hands. In March of 1970—two years after the report was completed—a gay rights organization in Los Angeles called the ONE Institute held a lecture where the entire NIMH report was read aloud. It's not clear how this group got ahold of the report, but it's highly likely that Evelyn leaked it to them. She was connected to that community, and she was committed to changing people's minds about how they were perceived. As each recommendation was read, there was rising excitement in the room. This was a document that could radically change the direction of the gay rights movement! And yet, upon hearing that the NIMH chose to sit on the report for two years, the room erupted in frustration and anger. The group decided unanimously to take matters into their own hands and, without authorization from the NIMH, disseminate the report themselves. It was published in the ONE Institute Quarterly, a journal devoted to "homophile studies" (the study of same-sex attraction), in 1970.

W. Dorr Legg, editor of the ONE Institute Quarterly, said in his introduction to the report, "Clearcut calls for action occur throughout its pages in terms which only a few years earlier would have seemed highly improbable as coming from a body with government sponsorship." He then went on to chastise the government for suppressing the report: "That so important a text might be allowed to quietly sink out of sight and be forgotten began to seem a distinct possibility." [17]

This little journal certainly didn't have the readership of a major publication like The New York Times. However, it did reach people who were ready to take action in a much bigger way. The release of this report—coupled with the knowledge that it was being suppressed by the government—was exactly the catalyst the gay liberation movement needed.

They were ready to roll up their sleeves and fight for the declassification of "homosexuality" as a mental disorder.

᠅

YOU MAY TAKE THIS AS A DECLARATION OF WAR AGAINST YOU

When gay activist Frank Kameny shouted this into the microphone to a roomful of psychiatrists, it marked a radical shift in the fight for gay rights. Throughout the 1950s and early 1960s, leaders of gay rights groups like the Mattachine Society (including Kameny himself) told their members that the best way to convince people that gay people were normal was to, well, act normal. When they protested, they did so quietly, holding signs and marching silently. The men, clean-shaven and sporting fresh haircuts, wore suits and ties. The women wore dresses, heels, and makeup. They reasoned that if they looked like everyone else, they might actually be treated with respect.

As time progressed, it became clear that the "button up and look good" approach wasn't working. Gay activists were tired of playing nice, especially as the police continued to raid gay bars, arrest their patrons, and throw them in jail. They were also sick of being labeled as "sick" and forced to undergo barbaric treatments to make them straight. In 1969, this anger and frustration culminated in the Stonewall riots, a multi-day series of violent protests triggered by a routine police raid at the Stonewall Inn in New York City. After that event, gay activists tossed their suits and dresses aside, raised their voices, and took to the streets. Now the goal was to disrupt the status quo, using various forms of civil disobedience.

Kameny was a key leader in the early gay rights movement. During the Red Scare, Kameny was fired from his job as an astronomer with the U.S. Army because of his sexual orientation. After that, he worked tirelessly on behalf of the gay community, advocating for their rights. And one of the issues he took up was the labeling of "homosexuality" as a psychiatric disorder.

Once the gay community learned about the NIMH Task Force report—and the fact that its contents had been squelched by the government—they were infuriated, and ready to do battle in a different way. Their first target was the 1970 American Psychiatric Association conference in San Francisco. Bieber was in attendance, presenting his theories about the diagnosis and treatment of same-sex attraction and sexual behaviors. Activists who were not psychiatrists snuck into the conference, showed up at

Bieber's talk, and disrupted the session by interrupting the speakers, shouting them down, and engaging in public ridicule.

That action got the American Psychiatric Association's attention, and in 1971, Kameny and longtime lesbian activist Barbara Gittings were invited to a session titled "Gay is Good." During that session, many psychiatrists heard for the first time how stigmatizing it was for gay and lesbian people to be labeled with a psychiatric diagnosis. At one point, Kameny took the microphone and yelled, "Psychiatry is the enemy incarnate. Psychiatry has waged a relentless war of extermination against us. You may take this as a declaration of war against you."[18] Kameny also collaborated with the Gay Liberation Front, a radical activist group that was formed in the wake of the Stonewall riots, to engage in more widespread anti-psychiatry protests. The gay activists joined forces with anti-psychiatry activists, a group who questioned the legitimacy of psychiatric diagnoses in general, and jointly protested the meetings. It was clear that the gay community wasn't willing to be messed with anymore, and they were ready for a fight.

In 1972, the American Psychiatric Association finally agreed to host a session titled "Psychiatry: Friend or Foe to the Homosexual? A Dialogue." Both

Kameny and Gittings participated. Dr. Judd Marmor, a straight psychiatrist who had served with Evelyn on the NIMH Task Force, was also asked to participate. Once the panel was formed, Kay Lahusen, who was Gittings' partner, noted that while the panel had gay and lesbian activists as well as a psychiatrist, they needed to find someone who was both gay *and* a psychiatrist to participate. Gittings asked a number of people if they would join the panel, but none were willing to reveal in such a public forum the fact that they were gay. She played with some other ideas, like reading letters from gay psychiatrists without revealing their names, but didn't think that would have enough of an impact. Then Gittings decided to ask one more person.

That person was John Fryer, a psychiatrist who was gay. Fryer was a professor at Temple University but wasn't yet tenured and didn't have job security. He had already lost two jobs because of his sexual orientation, one at the University of Pennsylvania, the other at Friends Hospital, a psychiatric facility in Philadelphia. The administrator at Friends Hospital who fired him had said, "If you were gay and not flamboyant, we would keep you. If you were flamboyant and not gay we would keep you. But since you are both gay and flamboyant, we cannot keep you." Fryer, not surprisingly, was very worried about getting fired a third time, and was hesitant about having any part in the panel.

The solution? A disguise. Fryer was listed in the schedule as "Dr. H. Anonymous" (the "H" stood for "Henry"). He appeared on the panel wearing a rubber mask that looked like a cross between Richard Nixon and a horror movie villain, a bushy wig, and an oversized tuxedo with velvet-edged lapels. Fryer's partner, an actor and drama major, helped him put together the outrageous getup. Speaking through a microphone that distorted his voice, Dr. Anonymous began his remarks.

"I am a homosexual. I am a psychiatrist." This marked the first time a psychiatrist had disclosed his sexual orientation on such a public stage. He then went on to note that the American Psychiatric Association had, in fact, many gay psychiatrists, all of whom had to hide their identities from their colleagues for fear of discrimination. Dr. Anonymous also pointed out that, because the gay community had such a deep mistrust of the field of psychiatry, many gay psychiatrists had to lie to their friends about what they did for a living. He identified the need for psychiatrists to challenge prejudice and discrimination, and the need to shift away from considering homosexuality to be a disorder. Ironically, one of the audience members sitting in the front row

The Mask

You,
in the front row.

I see you sitting there
staring at me.

Do I look like a villain in a slasher film,
my grotesque face melting before your eyes?

Are you afraid that poisonous snakes
will jump out of my hair and bite you?

Has the haunted house smell of my velvet tux
tunneled its musty stench up through your nostrils?

Does my crank caller voice
sound like an abductor demanding ransom?

I see your eyes screaming in terror.
I see your hands writhing in fear.

But if you actually looked into my eyes,
twinkling right in front of you,

and if you actually looked at my hands,
the ones you used to shake every day,

you'd see
who I really am.

And you'd be reminded
that the man inside this getup

frightens you far more
than any costume ever could.

was the administrator who had fired Fryer from his
job at Friends Hospital. He never once realized that
Dr. Anonymous was, in fact, his former employee.

Years later, in 2002, Dr. Jack Drescher, who was
the chair of the American Psychiatric Association's
Committee on Gay, Lesbian, and Bisexual Issues,
commented on "[t]he irony ... that an openly homosexual psychiatrist had to wear a mask to protect
his career. So the fact that someone would get up
on stage, even in disguise, at the risk of professional
denunciation or loss of job, it was not a small thing.
Even in disguise, it was a very, very brave thing to do."

After the panel discussion, Dr. Anonymous,
still using a voice disguiser, was interviewed for a
local radio talk show. The broadcast took place from
one of the gay bars in the area. While some of his
friends and colleagues knew at the time that Fryer
was Dr. Anonymous, Fryer didn't publicly disclose
having played the role of Dr. Anonymous until the
American Psychiatric Association's 1994 convention
in Philadelphia.

The panel didn't immediately change the minds
of the American Psychiatric Association leaders, and
homosexuality remained a diagnosis—for a while.
However, Gittings later said, "His speech shook
up psychiatry. He was the right person at the right
time." Even though his performance didn't result in

instantaneous change, it did plant some seeds in the minds of psychiatrists with influence and clout.

☆

All the protests and panels got the American Psychiatric Association's attention. While activists were swarming the halls of the American Psychiatric Association conventions and demanding change, the organization's leaders were debating what to do. Should "homosexuality" remain a psychiatric disorder, should it be re-classified as something else, or should it be removed altogether? Although conversations were happening in closed-door sessions, no formal actions took place until 1973. American Psychiatric Association leaders decided to host a formal debate at that year's annual convention, titled "Should Homosexuality be in the APA's Nomenclature?" People from both sides of the issue were invited to share their perspectives.

Meanwhile, the American Psychiatric Association's Nomenclature Committee was also hard at work. This was the group tasked with making recommendations regarding what constitutes a mental disorder, and whether certain conditions should be included in the DSM. The committee decided to create a sub-committee looking into the issue of "homosexuality".

Psychiatrist Robert Spitzer chaired that subcommittee, and the group came to the agreement that same-sex attraction, in and of itself, did not fit the definition of a mental disorder. Any distress that a gay person experienced wasn't necessarily caused by their sexual orientation, but rather by the prejudice and discrimination they faced by society. Spitzer's subcommittee brought their recommendations to several other American Psychiatric Association committees and deliberative bodies for review. In December of 1973, the recommendation to remove "homosexuality" from the DSM was brought to the American Psychiatric Association's Board of Trustees, who voted to accept the recommendation.

Psychiatrists like Bieber were very unhappy with this decision. At the time, Bieber was the American Psychiatric Association's research chair on "homosexuality," and the decision made by the Board of Trustees went against everything he believed. The following week, the New York Times published a conversation between Spitzer and Bieber on this issue. Going back and forth like a tennis match, Spitzer and Bieber sparred over what a diagnosable disorder is—and whether "homosexuality" fits into that category. From Spitzer's standpoint, if a person is happy with their sexual orientation, and if it's not causing any distress, then why treat it? Bieber, in contrast, took a very different perspective, comparing same-sex attraction and sexual behavior to polio: "Are you going to say this is normal? That a person who has legs that have been actually paralyzed by polio is a normal person even though the polio is no longer active?"[19] (Today, people who are disability activists would likely have something to say about this.)

Bieber's biggest complaint was that the Board of Trustees made a decision, rather than putting the question to a general vote of the membership. Bieber, Socarides, and others who opposed the vote circulated a petition urging the American Psychiatric Association to take a popular vote. The American Psychiatric Association conceded. Out of 10,000 voting members, 58% voted to uphold the decision made by the Board of Trustees.[20]

This was a huge win for the gay community. But it didn't mean that "homosexuality" was removed entirely from the DSM. Instead, it was now considered to be a "Sexual Orientation Disturbance" (SOD), which was diagnosed only if the person was distressed by their same-sex attractions and wanted to change. While this modification greatly reduced the number of gay people subjected to involuntary and barbaric treatments, it still allowed for conversion therapies.

In 1980, when the third edition of the DSM was released, the term "Sexual Orientation Disturbance" was replaced by a term called "Ego-Dystonic Homosexuality" (which essentially means that a person is unhappy about being gay). But critics called this into question, using some potent analogies: What if a person of color is distressed by their skin color, or their hair texture, or their facial features? Should that person be diagnosed with a disorder? What about a person who is short, and would rather be tall? Is that person mentally ill? People recognized that pathologizing someone for having internalized society's prejudices about their identity was unfair.

By 1987—30 years after Evelyn Hooker published her groundbreaking study—the next revision of the DSM was released, and "Ego-Dystonic Homosexuality" was removed entirely. The American Psychiatric Association was finally taking a clear stand that same-sex attraction was in no way a mental disorder.

Epitaph

Homosexuality,
upon your death we are set free.
We bid you a cool farewell
knowing you will burn in hell.

Gestated for decades
Born 1952
Died 1973 (and again, in 1987)

Chapter 6

Grand Marshal

The decision to declassify "homosexuality" as a mental disorder had a ripple effect on the entire gay liberation movement. It was harder to justify arresting gay men and charging them with a criminal act, firing (or refusing to hire) people because of their sexual orientation, denying LGBTQ+ people the opportunity to serve in the military, or defining straight marriage as the only healthy type of relationship and family structure. While some of these forms of discrimination against LGBTQ+ people still exist, the LGBTQ+ rights movement has come a long way since 1973.

Evelyn, while a staunch supporter of LGBTQ+ rights, was always focused on the individuals who were affected by her research. "One of the great joys of my life is that I was able to do something for the ordinary man and woman," she said in an interview with the *Los Angeles Times*. In that same interview, she shared a story about a woman who had approached her at a party to thank her for her work. When her parents found out she was a lesbian, they responded by sending her to a mental institution known for using shock therapy, and this woman knew that's what she'd be in for. However, the doctor who was assigned to treat her had read Hooker's research, and he ultimately decided not to go through with the shock treatments. "I've wanted to meet you because I wanted to tell you what you saved me from," the woman said to Evelyn.

Ever since she'd returned from her trip to Berlin in the 1930s, she knew she wanted to find a way to stop intolerance and injustice, and promote acceptance. And as she listened to Sam From, she was determined to take on the responsibility of studying a marginalize, persecuted, and oppressed group of people. "[W]hat really brings joy to my heart is that somehow [my research] reached those people I wanted it to reach."[21]

What You Saved Me From

She was only
sixteen years old
when her parents found out.

They told her to get in the car
and they went for a long, long drive,
never stopping until they arrived.

The hospital looked
stark, drab, lifeless.
Just like the patients.

They'd had "aversive conditioning,"
which is code for
shocking the gay away.

The doctor's eyes lingered
on the medical journal.
He couldn't do it.

Years later,
she spotted a tall woman
across the room.

She walked up to her,
tears streaming down her face,
and said,

"I've wanted to meet you
because I wanted to tell you
what you saved me from."[22]

Sometimes it takes a while to see the impact of your efforts. In Evelyn's case, "a while" meant 30 years! Although Evelyn's work was trivialized in the late 1950s and 1960s, it was ultimately the study that catalyzed change for the LGBTQ+ community. Her research was pivotal in the decision to remove the "homosexuality" diagnosis from the DSM, and it was after that occurred in 1987 that her work became much more widely known, both within and outside of the LGBTQ+ community.

Evelyn didn't do her research so she could win awards. But people wanted to honor and thank her for the work she'd done, and the way she'd changed their lives. The first official award she received came from the Los Angeles Gay and Lesbian Community Services Center in December of 1989. She was awarded the organization's highest honor, the Morris Kight Humanitarian Award, "for her compassion, foresight, intelligence and tenacity which has enriched and improved the quality of life for all lesbians and gay men."

In 1991, the American Psychological Association awarded Evelyn with the Award for Distinguished Contribution to Psychology in the Public Interest—a major recognition and honor. The official announcement read as follows:

"When homosexuals were
considered to be mentally ill,
were forced out of government
jobs, and were arrested in
police raids, Evelyn Hooker
courageously sought and
obtained research support
from the National Institute
of Mental Health (NIMH) to
compare a matched sample of
homosexual and heterosexual
men. Her pioneering study,
published in 1957, challenged
the widespread belief
that homosexuality is a
pathology by demonstrating
that experienced clinicians
using psychological tests
widely believed at the time
to be appropriate could not
identify the nonclinical
homosexual group. This
revolutionary study provided
empirical evidence that

normal homosexuals existed,
and supported the radical
idea then emerging that
homosexuality is within
the normal range of human
behavior. Despite the stigma
associated with homosexuality,
she received an NIMH Research
Career Award in 1961 to
continue her work. In 1967, she
became chair of the NIMH Task
Force on Homosexuality, which
provided a stamp of validation
and research support for
other major empirical
studies. Her research,
leadership, mentorship, and
tireless advocacy for an
accurate scientific view of
homosexuality for more than
three decades has been an
outstanding contribution
to psychology in the public
interest."[23]

The following year, in 1992, Evelyn received the Lifetime Achievement Award from the American Psychological Association, the most prestigious award a psychologist can receive. That same year, the documentary film *Changing Our Minds: The Story of Evelyn Hooker* was released. It was nominated for an Academy Award.

Evelyn was honored in ways that went far beyond certificates and plaques. Shortly before his death, one of her former research participants, Wayne Placek, contacted Evelyn to thank her for the work she'd done, and to inform her that he planned to give her a large inheritance—enough to fund psychological research on LGBTQ+ people for many, many years. Evelyn didn't remember Placek, but learned that he was very involved in the Los Angeles gay community, particularly at ONE, Inc. Placek asked Evelyn to take the lead on establishing the fund, locating a permanent home for it, and developing protocols for receiving grant applications, evaluating those requests, and allocating funds to researchers studying LGBTQ+ issues. Placek died in 1994, and the first Wayne Placek awards were granted in 1995 by the American Psychological Foundation. These grants are still being awarded today.

Evelyn appreciated all the recognition from professional organizations. But probably one of her most cherished opportunities came from the gay community itself. On June 22, 1986, Evelyn, sitting in the back seat of a convertible, waved to the crowds as the Grand Marshal of the Christopher Street West Gay Pride Parade (now known as Los Angeles Pride).

In the LGBTQ+ community, being elected Grand Marshal of a Pride parade is one of the most significant tributes a person can receive. It's a sign of deep respect, reverence, and veneration. Evelyn, lightheartedly referred to as the "Grande Dame of the Gay Community,"[24] beamed from ear to ear as the car traveled through the heart of the "gayborhood," down Santa Monica Boulevard through West Hollywood.

Evelyn died at her home in Santa Monica on November 18, 1996.

Grand Marshal

Today's the day!
Welcome to the "gay"borhood,
out here in West Hollywood!
With arched balloons and rainbow flags
and glittered, sequined queens in drag.

Here she comes!
The Grande Dame of the Boulevard,
the empress of the avant-garde,
winding down the promenade
behind the revving motorcade.

It's the moment we've been waiting for!
She's riding in her classic car
and waving like a movie star
cruising past the royal palms
showered with confetti bombs.

There she is!
The Grand Marshal of our parade!
The classiest of renegades,
she's now arriving on the scene!
Your royal majesty, the Queen!

How shall we honor thee?
Let us count the ways!

TIMELINE

May 1897: Magnus Hirschfeld founds the
Scientific–Humanitarian Committee, the first
LGBTQ+ rights organization in the world,
in Berlin.

September 2, 1907: Evelyn Gentry (to
become Evelyn Hooker) is born in North Platte,
Nebraska.

1917: *The Homosexuality of Men and Women* by
Magnus Hirschfeld is published.

July 6, 1919: Magnus Hirschfeld opens the
Institute for Sexual Research.

1920: The 19th Amendment to the U.S.
Constitution is ratified, giving White women
the right to vote.

Fall 1924: Evelyn starts college at the University
of Colorado at Boulder, a school that now awards
the Dr. Evelyn Hooker Advocacy Award annually
to a faculty member who mentors LGBTQ+
students.

1930: Sigmund Freud signs a petition opposing the criminalization and treatment of "homosexuality."

1932: Evelyn earns her PhD from Johns Hopkins University.

May 10, 1933: Nazis burn the thousands of materials in the archives of the Institute for Sexual Research in Berlin.

1934: Evelyn contracts tuberculosis.

1935: Professor Louis Max presents his paper at the American Psychological Association conference titled *Breaking Up a Homosexual Fixation by the Conditional Reaction Technique*.

1936: Dr. Walter Freeman begins performing lobotomies (and goes on to perform thousands of them for the next several years).

1937: Evelyn receives a fellowship to Berlin Institute of Psychotherapy and lives in Germany with a Jewish host family until 1938.

November 9–10, 1938: Kristallnacht, "The Night of the Broken Glass," takes place, in which Nazis attacked Jewish people in Germany.

1945: World War II ends. During the war, six million Jewish people were killed, including Evelyn's former host family. Several other groups were also persecuted, including gay people as sexual criminals. Thousands of men in concentration camps were killed for being gay, as well as an unknown number of women for being lesbian.

April 8, 1947: Dr. Alfred Kinsey founds the Institute for Sex Research (now named the Kinsey Institute for Sex Research).

June 1948: Congress passes a law "to provide for the treatment of sexual psychopaths in the District of Columbia"—"homosexuality" was included as something that defines a "sexual psychopath."

1948: *Sexual Behavior in the Human Male* by Alfred Kinsey is published.

February 9, 1950: Senator Joseph McCarthy adds fuel to the Red Scare in a speech in West Virginia.

June 7, 1950: Congress approves a resolution to conduct a more thorough investigation of "the alleged employment by the departments and agencies of the Government of homosexuals and other moral perverts," beginning the Lavender Scare.

November 11, 1950: The Mattachine Society, an early American gay rights organization, meets for the first time.

December 1950: The report *Employment of Homosexuals and Other Sex Perverts in Government* is issued, concluding that "homosexuals" should not be employed by the federal government because they were "generally unsuitable" and constituted "security risks."

1951: Evelyn marries Edward Hooker.

April 27, 1953: President Dwight D. Eisenhower signs Executive Order 10450, which established security requirements for people who wanted to work for the U.S. government. Because gay people were automatically viewed as a security threat, this executive order prevented them from getting a government job.

Timeline

1953: Evelyn applies for a grant from the National Institute of Mental Health (NIMH) to fund her study on "homosexuality."

October 20, 1956: Evelyn's paper asserting that "homosexuality" is not a disorder, titled *The Adjustment of the Male Overt Homosexual,* is published in the Journal of Projective Techniques.

1957: Frank Kameny is fired from his federal job with the Army Map Service for being gay.

1961: The film *Boys Beware* is released.

1961: Evelyn receives the NIMH Research Career Award.

June 26, 1964: Two articles in an issue of *LIFE* magazine depict gay people in a negative light.

March 7, 1967: "The Homosexuals," an episode of *CBS Reports,* airs.

1967: The director of NIMH asks Evelyn to work on a special task force to come up with recommendations for the NIMH regarding what to do about homosexuality.

1968: *The Overt Homosexual* by Irving Bieber is published.

June 28, 1969: The Stonewall Riots, an important turning point in the movement for sexual and gender minorities to win equality, begin.

October 10, 1969: The NIMH Task Force on Homosexuality makes the recommendation to shift treatment efforts away from trying to change a person's sexual orientation, instead focusing on helping people be happy and well-adjusted. NIMH officials decide to delay reporting the recommendations.

March 1970: ONE Institute holds a lecture in Los Angeles where the entire NIMH Task Force report is read aloud. In the same month, ONE Institute Quarterly publishes the task force's report without authorization from NIMH.

1970: Evelyn retires from UCLA.

1971: Frank Kameny and Barbara Gittings are invited to an American Psychiatric Association session titled *Gay is Good* where Kameny says "Psychiatry is the enemy incarnate. Psychiatry has waged a relentless war of extermination against us. You may take this as a declaration of war against you."

1972: The American Psychiatric Association hosts a session about "homosexuality" titled *Psychiatry: Friend or Foe to the Homosexual? A Dialogue* where Dr. H. Anonymous (now known to have been Dr. John E. Fryer) delivers remarks in a mask.

1973: The American Psychiatric Association hosts a debate called *Should Homosexuality Be in the APA's Nomenclature?*

December 1973: The American Psychiatric Association's Board of Trustees votes to accept the recommendation to remove "homosexuality" from the DSM replacing it with "Sexual Orientation Disturbance."

October 14, 1979: The first National March on Washington for Lesbian and Gay Rights takes place in Washington, DC.

1980: The new edition of the DSM is released, in which the term "Sexual Orientation Disturbance" is replaced by "Ego-Dystonic Homosexuality."

June 22, 1986: Evelyn serves as Grand Marshal of the Christopher Street West Gay Pride Parade (now known as Los Angeles Pride).

1987: The next revision of the DSM is released, in which "Ego-Dystonic Homosexuality" is removed.

December 1989: Evelyn receives the Morris Kight Humanitarian Award from the Los Angeles Gay and Lesbian Community Services Center.

1991: Evelyn receives the Award for Distinguished Contribution to Psychology in the Public Interest from the American Psychological Association.

1992: Evelyn receives the Lifetime Achievement Award from the American Psychological Association.

November 18, 1996: Evelyn dies in Santa Monica, California, at the age of 89.

June 26, 2003: The U.S. Supreme Court decriminalizes sex between two people of the same sex.

June 26, 2015: The U.S. Supreme Court legalizes same-sex marriage.

DISCUSSION QUESTIONS

1. Evelyn took many risks to stand up for a community she wasn't a part of when it would have been easier to study something else. Why do you think she did this? Would you do this? What would hold you back from taking the risks she did?

2. Where did most straight Americans get their information about gay Americans before the 1970s? What might have been different if those sources had told a different side of the story? What responsibility does the media have to tell unbiased stories even if the majority believe in the bias?

3. LGBTQ+ people experienced discrimination in the legal, political, psychological, and religious spheres, as well as many others. How did the different spheres of discrimination influence each other? For example, if gay people legally had equal rights, do you think that would have helped them to be treated fairly in psychology?

4. When asking politely and other calm methods of trying to achieve equality didn't work, the gay rights movement started more radical approaches and yelled at people and took to the streets. Would you do the same thing in that situation? Can you think of other movements that had similar evolutions?

5. Intersecting identities like race and class cause people to have different experiences. How do you think some of these affected LGBTQ+ people of the time. How do they still affect LGBTQ+ people? What intersecting identities do you have? (For example, you have a gender, race, class, sexual orientation, physical ability, immigration status, religion, etc.). How do those identities add up into how you experience the world?

6. How did fear of what people don't understand play into how straight Americans treated gay Americans? How does that same fear affect other communities in the US today? How can learning about communities different from us make society fairer for everyone?

How to Be an LGBTQ+ Ally

Evelyn Hooker wasn't gay, but she helped gay people live better lives through her actions. That's what an ally does—advocate on behalf of a group they're not a part of.

Someone inside the LGBTQ+ community who advocates for gay rights isn't an ally; they are an activist. You have to be outside of the group to be an ally. The word comes from war talk—your ally in a war is not your own armed forces, but forces that fight on the same side as you against a common enemy.

So, how can you be an ally to people like the ones in this book that Evelyn helped? First, you need to understand who they are.

Be Inclusive

While this book talks mainly about gay people, because that was where the discussion was focused at the time, the LGBTQ+ community is made up of many more kinds of people than just gay and lesbian people. People who are bisexual, pansexual, transgender, non-binary, queer, asexual, agender, and many other identities all are part of a community together because they all have sexualities and genders that are not considered to be the "norm." LGBTQ+ people are every race, religion, gender, age, nationality, and more. To be an ally to one, you should be an ally to the whole extended community.

Be A Follower

Being an ally is often about listening. Allies don't tell their LGBTQ+ friends what they should do or how to do it; they help their friends carry out what their friends want. Allies can help their LGBTQ+ friends by amplifying their voices, donating to their causes, showing up to demonstrations, and contacting legislators on their behalf. They don't say what the demonstrations should be or what donations should be used for, they just help where they are needed and follow the direction of the group they want to help.

Be Proactive

While following is important in many situations, so is taking initiative in other contexts. For example, don't expect an LGBTQ+ person to explain everything about being LGBTQ+ to you—try to do your own research before asking LGBTQ+ people to give their time and energy to explain what could also be found online or in books like this. If you must ask, be mindful of your question and consider if it is appropriate or how it may make an LGBTQ+ person feel (for example, ask for personal pronouns, not for a birth name). It's also the job of an ally to speak up for LGBTQ+ people in a situation where someone says something mean or incorrect about them. You can speak up while still not speaking over or instead of LGBTQ+ people.

Be A Student

Learn from your mistakes and realize that you'll always be learning. Sometimes you'll stretch yourself to learn about things that make you uncomfortable, like hearing about the real-life discrimination LGBTQ+ people go through, but educating yourself (while maintaining your own boundaries and self-care) is important. Learn about LGBTQ+ history, gender-neutral pronouns, and current issues important to the LGBTQ+ community. When you make a mistake, own it, apologize, and move on.

Be A Friend

Like you would for anyone, be a kind friend to LGBTQ+ people around you. Listen, offer support, respect people's pronouns and identities, and show up when you're asked to. In the end, being an ally is being a friend.

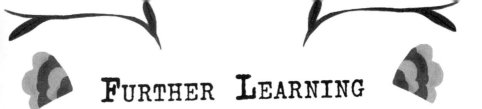

FURTHER LEARNING

Books

Bronski, M. (2019). *A queer history of the United States for young people* (adapted by R. Chevat). Beacon Press.

Dawson, J. (2015). *This book is gay.* Sourcebooks.

Ignotofsky, R. (2016). *Women in science: 50 fearless pioneers who changed the world.* Ten Speed Press.

Long, M. G. (2014). *Gay is good: The life and letters of gay rights pioneer Franklin Kameny.* Syracuse University Press.

Pohlen, J. (2015). *Gay & lesbian history for kids: The century-long struggle for LGBT rights.* Chicago Review Press.

Prager, S. (2020). *Rainbow revolutionaries: 50 LGBTQ+ people who made history.* HarperCollins.

Reimer, M. & Brown, L. (2019). *We are everywhere: Protest, power, and pride in the history of queer liberation.* Ten Speed Press.

Documentaries

Sammon, P. & Singer, B. (Directors). (2020). *Cured* [Film]. Singer & Deschamps Productions and Story Center Films.

Schiller, G. (Director), & Rosenberg, R. (Co-Director). (1984). *Before Stonewall: The making of a gay and lesbian community* [Film]. Alternative Media Information Center, Center for the Study of Filmed History, and Before Stonewall, Inc.

Schmiechen, R. (Director). (1991). *Changing our minds: The story of Dr. Evelyn Hooker* [Film]. Intrepid Productions.

Dupre, J. (Director). (1998). *Out of the past* [Film]. Allumination Filmworks, LLC.

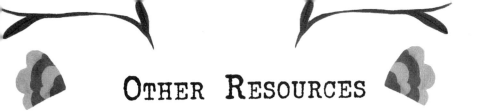

Other Resources

American Psychological Association's Office on Sexual Orientation and Gender Diversity
apa.org/pi/lgbt

Family Acceptance Project
familyproject.sfsu.edu

GLMA: Health Professionals Advancing LGBTQ Equality
glma.org

GLSEN: Championing LGBTQ issues in K–12 Education
glsen.org

It Gets Better Project
itgetsbetter.org

ONE Archives Foundation
onearchives.org

oSTEM: Out in Science, Technology, Engineering, and Mathematics
ostem.org

PFLAG: The Nation's Largest Family and Ally Organization
pflag.org

Quist
quistapp.com

Trevor Project
thetrevorproject.org

ENDNOTES

1–4.   Minton, H. L. (2001). *Departing from deviance.* University of Chicago Press.

5.   Morgan, J. J. B. (1928). *The psychology of abnormal people.* Longmans, Green & Co.

6.   Ordover, N. (2003). *American eugenics: Race, queer anatomy, and the science of nationalism.* University of Minnesota Press.

7.   Anderson, J. S. (2018, August 5). Why we still haven't banished conversion therapy in 2018. *The Washington Post.* https://www.washingtonpost.com/news/made-by-history/wp/2018/08/05/why-we-still-havent-banished-conversion-therapy-in-2018/

8.   Cordingley, G. E. (2005). *Walter Freeman's lobotomies at Athens State Hospital.* Cordinley Neurology. https://www.cordingleyneurology.com/lobotomies.html

9.   Scot, Jamie (2013, June 28). *Shock the gay away: Secrets of early gay aversion therapy revealed.* HuffPost. https://www.huffpost.com/entry/shock-the-gay-away-secrets-of-early-gay-aversion-therapy-revealed_b_3497435

10. United States. (1948). *Laws and concurrent resolutions enacted during the second session of the eightieth congress of the United States of America.* https://www.loc.gov/law/help/statutes-at-large/80th-congress/c80s2.pdf

11. United States. (1950). *Employment of homosexuals and other sex perverts in government: Interim report submitted to the Committee on Expenditures in the Executive Departments by its Subcommittee on Investigations pursuant to S. Res. 280, 81st Congress, a resolution authorizing the Committee on Expenditures in the Executive Departments to carry out certain duties.* https://diogenesii.files.wordpress.com/2012/11/employment-of-homosexuals-and-other-sex-perverts-in-govt.pdf

12. Hooker, E. (1993). *Reflections of a 40-year exploration: A scientific view on homosexuality.* UC Davis. https://psychology.ucdavis.edu/rainbow/html/hooker_address.html

13.–14. Shenitz, B. (1990, June 10). The grande dame of gay liberation: Evelyn Hooker's friendship with a UCLA student spurred her to studies that changed the way psychiatrists view homosexuality. *Los Angeles Times.* https://www.

latimes.com/archives/la-xpm-1990-06-10-tm-539-
story.html

15. Williams, T. (2013). *Mysterious something in the light:
The life of Raymond Chandler.* Chicago Review Press.

16. Welch, P. (1964, June 26). Homosexuality in
America. *LIFE Magazine.* https://books.google.com/
books?id=qEEEAAAAMBAJ&pg=PA66&source=gbs_
toc_r&cad=2#v=onepage&q&f=false

17. ONE Institute of Homophile Studies. (1970). One
Institute quarterly: Homophile studies.

18. Drescher, J. (2015). Out of DSM: Depathologizing
homosexuality. *Behavioral Sciences, 5*(4), 565–575.
https://doi.org/10.3390/bs5040565

19. Johnston, D. (1973, December 23). The APA ruling
on homosexuality. *The New York Times.* https://
www.nytimes.com/1973/12/23/archives/the-
issue-is-subtle-the-debate-still-on-the-apa-ruling-
on.html

20. Drescher, J. (2015). Out of DSM: Depathologizing
homosexuality. *Behavioral Sciences, 5*(4), 565–575.
https://doi.org/10.3390/bs5040565

21. Shenitz, B. (1990, June 10). The grande dame of gay
liberation: Evelyn Hooker's friendship with a UCLA

student spurred her to studies that changed the way psychiatrists view homosexuality. *Los Angeles Times*. https://www.latimes.com/archives/la-xpm-1990-06-10-tm-539-story.html

22.   Marcus, E. (Host). (2016–present). Dr. Evelyn Hooker [Audio podcast]. *Making Gay History*. https://makinggayhistory.com/podcast/episode-1-4/

23.   Awards for distinguished contribution to psychology in the public interest (1992). *American Psychologist, 47*(4), 498–503. https://doi.org/10.1037/h0090776

24.   Shenitz, B. (1990, June 10). The grande dame of gay liberation: Evelyn Hooker's friendship with a UCLA student spurred her to studies that changed the way psychiatrists view homosexuality. *Los Angeles Times*. https://www.latimes.com/archives/la-xpm-1990-06-10-tm-539-story.html

Gayle E. Pitman, PhD, is a professor of psychology and women's studies at Sacramento City College. Her teaching and writing focuses on gender and sexual orientation, and she has worked extensively with the LGBTQ+ community. She is the author of *My Maddy*, *This Day in June*, *When You Look Out the Window*, *Feminism From A to Z*, and *Sewing the Rainbow*. *This Day in June* was the winner of 2015 Stonewall Book Award: Mike Morgan and Larry Romans Children's & Young Adult Literature Award and a Top Ten Title on the ALA Rainbow List. In 2021, it was named as a top 10 Most Challenged Books of the decade by ALA's Office of Intellectual Freedom. Gayle lives in California. Visit gaylepitman.com, @GaylePitmanAuthor on Facebook, and @GaylePitman on Twitter and Instagram.

Sarah Prager is the author of three books for young people on LGBTQ+ history: *Queer, There, and Everywhere: 23 People Who Changed the World*, *Rainbow Revolutionaries: 50 LGBTQ+ People Who Made History*, and *Kind Like Marsha: Learning from LGBTQ+ Leaders*. Her writing has also appeared in the New York Times, The Atlantic, National Geographic, and many other outlets. She speaks on LGBTQ+ history to groups around the world. Visit sarahprager.com.

Sarah Green is an illustrator and designer from San Francisco. She graduated from Rhode Island School of Design in 2014. She lives in San Francisco, California, and Vancouver, Canada. Visit sarahgreenillustration. com, @s_green_bean on Twitter, and @sarahgreenstudio on Instagram.

Magination Press is the children's book imprint of the American Psychological Association. APA works to advance psychology as a science and profession and as a means of promoting health and human welfare. Magination Press books reach young readers and their parents and caregivers to make navigating life's challenges a little easier. It's the combined power of psychology and literature that makes a Magination Press book special. Visit maginationpress.org and @MaginationPress on Facebook, Twitter, Instagram, and Pinterest.